ANDEAN INS
KNITS

Designs in Luxurious Alpaca

HELEN HAMANN

INTERWEAVE PRESS
www.interweave.com

Photo courtesy: Heinz/PromPerú

TO MY FATHER

Editor: Ann Budd
Technical Editor: Lori Gayle
Design: Paulette Livers
Production: Dean Howes
Photo styling: Paulette Livers, Ann Swanson
Illustrations: Gayle Ford
Photography: Joe Coca, unless otherwise noted
Proofreading and indexing: Nancy Arndt

Interweave Press LLC
201 East Fourth Street
Loveland, CO 80537-5655 USA
www.interweave.com

Printed and bound in China by Pimlico Book International

Library of Congress Cataloging-in-Publication Data

Hamann, Helen, 1954-
  Andean inspired knits : designs in luxurious alpaca /
Helen Hamann, author.
     p. cm.
  Includes bibliographical references and index.
    ISBN-13: 978-1-931499-93-4 (paperbound)
    ISBN-10: 1-931499-93-4 (paperbound)
  1. Knitting—Peru. 2. Alpaca (Textile) I. Title.
TT819.P4H36 2006
746.43'20432—dc22

                        2006002417

10 9 8 7 6 5 4 3 2 1

Photographs of historic textiles were generously provided by the
following sources:

Pages 3 and 58: Museo Nacional de Arqueologia y Anthropologia
e History del Peru.

Pages 13, 21, 23, 49, 59, 107, and 113: *Tejidos Milenarios del Peru*
by Jose Antonio de Lavalle and Rosario de Lavalle de Cardenas.
AFP Integra, 1999.

Page 33: *Huari* by Jose Antonio de Lavalle. Coleccion Arte y
Tesoros del Peru. Lima: Banco de Credito del Peru en la Cultura,
1984.

Page 45: Juan B. Ambrosetti Ethnographic Museum, Buenos
Aires.

Pages 61, 65, 75, 85, and 91: Museo Armano.

Pages 79, 99, and 117: *Chancay* by Jose Antonio de Lavalle and
Werner Lang. Coleccion Arte y Tesoros del Peru. Lima: Banco de
Credito del Peru en la Cultura, 1982.

Photographs of alpacas on pages 3, 13, 23, 33, 45, 49, 61,
65, 75, 79, 85, 91, 99, 107, 113, and 117 copyright Ronald
Winsauer, Aurora Alpacas.

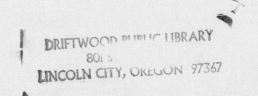

ACKNOWLEDGMENTS

I have to thank Lisa Hull and Tony Aguilar for their support and encouragement; the Dewhirst family for receiving me open-armed and making life so pleasant in beautiful Tennessee; German Freyre of Incalpaca for lending me the book *Ancient Peruvian Textiles* when I had exhausted all possibilities of buying a copy because it was out of print. I am also indebted to Jose Antonio de Lavalle for generously providing me with the photos of the textiles that appear in his books; PromPeru for the photos of Peru; Sharon Winsauer for developing instructions for lace stitches from photographs of textiles; Michell y Co. for generously providing yarn to make additional models; Alpaca with a Twist and Classic Elite Yarns for providing some exciting yarn colors to complement some of the designs; The Fibre Company who was willing and ready to custom-spin yarns for a few of the designs; Ronald Winsauer for providing the wonderful photos of alpacas. Special thanks to The Alpaca Yarn Company for providing the yarn for almost all of the designs from their large selection of colors and variety of yarns. My gratitude also to Carol Rapp and Betsy Whitehead, who helped me throughout the process.

This book would not have been possible without the vision, commitment, and dedication of the Interweave Press book team. In particular, Linda Stark for believing in me after a quick informal conversation and selling my dream to the rest of the team; Betsy Armstrong for assisting me in turning my wild thoughts into actual projects; Ann Budd for articulating my half-baked stories about alpacas and pre-Columbian textiles and translating them into proper English, eventually putting them all together in an entertaining and well-rounded text; and most of all Lori Gayle, who managed to decipher my rough notes into clear instructions. I'd like to also thank all the other members of the team who worked behind the scenes and with whom I had no personal contact, but whose expertise and artistry created this beautiful book.

CONTENTS

Introduction, 1

Embroidered Yoke Wrap and Crocheted Cloche, 2

Short Asymmetrical Jacket and Flower Pin, 12

PERUVIAN TEXTILES, 21

Long Asymmetrical Cardigan, 22

ALPACAS THROUGH THE AGES, 31

Patchwork Kimono and Beaded Cap, 32

Black and White Handbag, 44

Embroidered-Back Cardigan and Crocheted Beads, 48

CULTURAL EVOLUTION OF PERU, 58

Crocheted Poncho, 60

Short Cardigan with Ribbon Trim, 64

Lacy Shawl with Fur Trim, 74

Lliclla, 78

TRADITIONAL DRESS AND COSTUME, 83

Striped Pullover and Spiral Scarf, 84

Short Circular Cardigan, 90

Circular Cardigan with Tapestry Weaving, 98

Short Cape, 106

Geometric Scarf, 112

BREEDING ALPACAS TODAY, 115

Bolero, 116

Bohemian Poncho and Beret, 124

Glossary, 130

Bibliography, 137

Resources, 137

Index, 138

Photo, Helen Hamann

INTRODUCTION

The knitted designs in this book are inspired by the rich and varied pre-Columbian textiles, dating from about 500 B.C. to A.D. 1540, that were produced in the part of South America that is now Peru. The craftsmen (and women) who produced these textiles were accomplished spinners, dyers, and weavers, and had a superb sense of color and design. Even by today's standards, these textiles demonstrate skillful execution of intricate patterns.

Many of the best textiles were woven with fiber from the indigenous alpaca and its close relative, the llama. These docile animals produced thick coats of lustrous fiber for protection in the harsh highland environments. As far back as 3000 B.C., primitive cultures hunted these animals for food and used their hides as blankets and crude clothing. Over the next two thousand years, alpacas were domesticated so that their fiber could be spun and woven into textiles that were used for more sophisticated clothing, as well as currency and religious ceremonies. Alpacas continue to be bred for fiber in Peru and elsewhere in the world, and their fleece is universally considered one of the most luxurious fibers, being simultaneously warm, silky soft, easily dyed, water repellent, and anti-allergenic.

Each of the twenty-three projects in this book draws from an ancient textile pattern or motif, and each is executed in fine alpaca yarn. The projects are arranged roughly in chronological sequence according to the dates of the textiles that inspired them. From simple to complex, these garments and accessories represent thousands of years of Andean textile history and celebrate the unequaled luxury of the native alpaca.

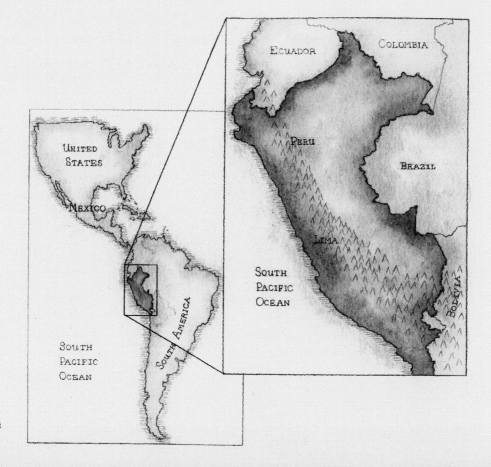

Opposite page, photo: Alejandro Balaguer/PromPerú

Embroidered Yoke Wrap and Crocheted Cloche

The inspiration for this unusual wrap came from a Paracas tapestry that dates from about 200 B.C. To draw attention to the embroidered flowers, I concentrated them along the yoke, which extends from the neck to the cuffs. The coordinating crocheted cloche is embellished with whimsical flowers.

Finished Size Wrap: About 60" (152.5 cm) wide from wrist to wrist, and 23" (58.5 cm) long at center back. Cloche: About 19½" (49.5 cm) circumference; will stretch to about 21" (53.5 cm).

Yarn CYCA #1 Super Fine (fingering weight). *Shown here:* The Fibre Company Fauna Black Lace (100% natural black baby alpaca; 175 yd [160 m]/ 50 g): black (MC), 14 skeins for wrap; 2 skeins for cloche.

CYCA #3 Light (DK). *Shown here:* Classic Elite Yarns Premiere (50% pima cotton, 50% Tencel; 108 yd [99 m]/50 g): #5275 coconut (tan), 1 skein for yoke embroidery.

DMC #3 Perle Cotton (100% cotton; 16 yd [15 m]/5 g): #742 gold, #718 magenta, #727 lemon, #340 periwinkle, #704 lime, and #519 light blue, 2 hanks each for yoke embroidery; 1 hank each for cloche flowers.

Needles Size 5 (3.75 mm): 32" (80 cm) circular (cir). Adjust needle size if necessary to obtain the correct gauge.

Notions Markers (m); removable marker or safety pin; tapestry needle; stitch holders; a few yards (meters) of waste yarn and smooth, satin ribbon for provisional cast-on; size C/2 (2.75 mm) crochet hook; size D/3 (3.25 mm) crochet hook (for cloche only); 1 yd (1 m) of 36" (90 cm) or wider fabric matching MC for yoke lining; ½ yd (.5 m) of 45" (115 cm) muslin for backing embroidered flowers; size 18 crewel needle for embroidering flowers; sharp-point sewing needle and matching thread for attaching lining; sewing pins; one 1¼" (3.2 cm) button.

Gauge 20½ sts and 24½ rows = 4" (10 cm) in St st using 2 strands of MC held tog for yoke; 22½ sts and 36 rows = 4" (10 cm) in garter st using single strand of MC for body. 13 sts and 13 rnds = 2" (5 cm) in single crochet worked in the rnd using 2 strands of MC held tog and smaller crochet hook.

Stitch Guide

Yoke Decreases: (RS rows) At beg of row, work k1, ssk; at end of row, knit to last 3 sts, k2tog, k1.

Yoke Increases: (RS rows) At beg of row, work k1, k1f&b (see Glossary, page 135); at end of row, knit to last 2 sts, k1f&b, k1.

Body Increases: (RS rows) At beg of row, work k2, k1f&b; at end of row, work to last 3 sts, k1f&b, k2.

Notes

- The yoke is worked first in a single piece with two strands of yarn for extra strength. The outlines of the stepped diamond motif are embroidered with a cotton/Tencel yarn, then the flowers are embroidered with mercerized cotton to add a shiny contrast to the inky, matte alpaca yarn.

- The garter-stitch body and "sleeves" are worked in two halves, each outward from the center back. The straight edge along the selvedge of the joined body halves is sewn to the back edge of the yoke with a pleat at the center of the back. Then the bound-off edges of the body are brought forward and sewn to the front edges of the yoke (see diagram, page 7). A single large button holds the wrap closed and lets the fabric drape gracefully around the contours of the body.

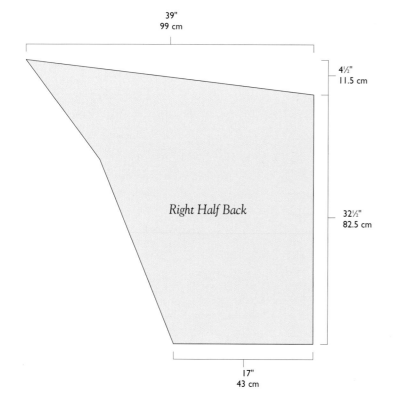

39"
99 cm

4½"
11.5 cm

Right Half Back

32½"
82.5 cm

17"
43 cm

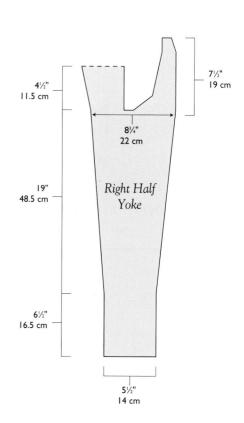

4½"
11.5 cm

7½"
19 cm

8¾"
22 cm

19"
48.5 cm

Right Half Yoke

6½"
16.5 cm

5½"
14 cm

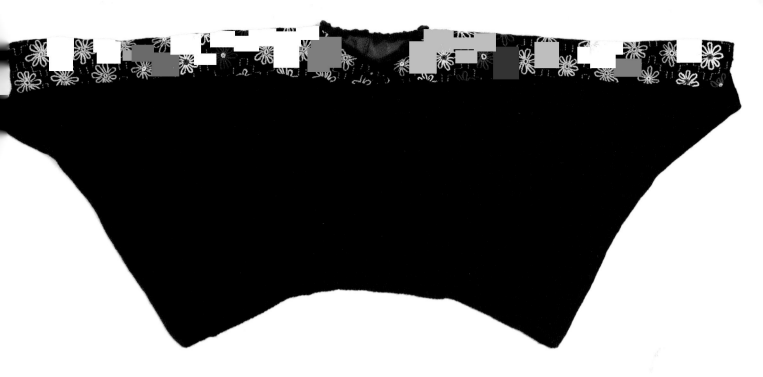

Yoke

Right Yoke

With double strand of MC, CO 28 sts. Work back and forth in St st until piece measures 6½" (16.5 cm; about 40 rows), ending with a WS row. Cont in St st for 116 more rows, ending with a WS row, and *at the same time* inc 1 st (see Stitch Guide) at beg of Rows 1, 21, 39, 51, 63, 75, 83, 95, and 107, and *also at the same time,* inc 1 st at end of Rows 21, 43, 63, 75, 87, 95, 103, 111, and 115—46 sts; 9 sts inc'd at each side; piece should measure about 25½" (65 cm) from CO.

Divide for Front and Back

(RS) K21 for front, BO 5 sts, knit to end for back—21 sts for front, 20 sts for back. Place 21 front sts on holder.

Back Yoke

Work 20 back sts even in St st for 3 rows, ending with a WS row. Work even in St st for 24 more rows, and *at the same time* dec 1 st (see Stitch Guide) at beg of Rows 3, 9, 15, and 21, and inc 1 st at end of Rows 5, 9, 13, 17, 19, and 23—22 sts; 4 sts dec'd at beg of RS rows; 6 sts inc'd at end of RS rows; piece measures about 4½" (11.5 cm) from where front and back yoke divided and about 30" (76 cm) from CO. Mark both ends of last row completed to indicate center of yoke. Work even in St st for 28 more rows, and *at the same time* inc 1 st at beg of Rows 5, 11, 17, and 23, and dec 1 st at end of Rows 3, 7, 9, 13, 17, and 21—20 sts rem; 4 sts inc'd at beg of RS rows and 6 sts dec'd at end of RS rows; piece measures about 9" (23 cm) from where front and back yoke divided. Place 20 back yoke sts on holder.

Right Front Yoke

Return 21 front sts to needle and rejoin double strand of yarn with WS facing. BO 2 sts at the beg of the next 2 WS rows—17 sts rem. Inc 1 st at beg of next RS row—18 sts. Beg with foll RS row, dec 1 st at end of row every 4 rows 6 times—12 sts rem; piece measures about 4½" (11.5 cm) from where

front and back yoke divided. Dec 1 st at beg of next RS row, then dec 1 st at end of foll RS row—10 sts. Work 3 rows even, then dec 1 st at *both* ends of next RS row—8 sts. [Work 3 rows even, BO 2 sts at beg of next RS row] 2 times—4 sts rem. Work 1 WS row even, then BO 2 sts at beg of next RS row—2 sts rem. Work 1 WS row even, then BO rem 2 sts—piece measures about 7½" (19 cm) from where front and back yoke divided.

Left Front Yoke

With double strand of yarn, CO 2 sts. Purl 1 WS row. Using the cable method (see Glossary, page 131), CO 2 sts at beg of next 2 RS rows—6 sts. Work 3 rows even. CO 2 sts at beg of next RS row—8 sts. Work 3 rows even. Inc 1 st at *both* ends of next RS row—10 sts. Work 3 rows even. Inc 1 st at end of next RS row, then inc 1 st at beg of foll RS row—12 sts. Work 1 WS row even. Beg with the next RS row, inc 1 st at end of row every 4th row 6 times—18 sts; 43 rows completed from CO; piece measures about 7" (18 cm) from CO. Dec 1 st at beg of next RS row—17 sts. Using the cable method, CO 2 sts at beg of next 2 WS rows—21 sts; 47 rows completed from CO; piece measures about 7½" (19 cm) from CO.

Left Yoke

K21 left front yoke sts, return 20 back yoke sts to left-hand needle with RS facing, use the cable method to CO 5 sts, knit across new sts, k20 back yoke sts to end—46 sts. Purl 1 WS row. Work in St st for 114 rows, ending with a WS row, and *at the same time* dec 1 st at beg of Rows 11, 23, 35, 43, 55, 67, 79, 97, and 115, and dec 1 st at end of Rows 1, 5, 13, 21, 29, 41, 53, 73, and 95—28 sts rem; piece measures about 19" (48.5 cm) from beg of left yoke. Work even in St st for 6½" (16.5 cm)—piece measures about 25½" (65 cm) from beg of left yoke, 30" (76 cm) from center back marker, and 60" (152.5 cm) from beg). BO all sts.

Edging

With smaller crochet hook for wrap and single strand of MC, work 1 row of rev single crochet (rev sc; see Glossary, page 132) around entire yoke, working 1 rev sc in each st and each row all the way around. Cut yarn and fasten off.

Neck Ruffle

With single strand of MC, WS of garment facing, and beg at point of left front yoke, pick up and knit 1 st for every row around neck opening to point of right front yoke, picking up just below the rev sc edging (crocheted yoke edging should remain free)—about 152 sts; exact st count is not critical. *Next row:* (RS) Work k1f&b in each st across—about 304 sts. Purl 1 row. *Next row:* (RS) *K1, yo; rep from * to end, ending k1 if you have an odd number of sts—about 608 sts. BO all sts, counting each yo as 1 st in the bind-off row.

Yoke Embroidery

With tan threaded on a tapestry needle and beg at marked center of yoke (indicated by heavy gridline on diagram), work outline of stepped diamond motifs using backstitch (see Glossary, page 133) according to Embroidery Diagram at right. *Note:* The diagram shows only the first few diamond motifs to get you started; continue the embroidery in pattern out to all the edges of the yoke; yoke shaping shown on embroidery diagram is approximate. Using perle cotton in flower colors as shown in illustration on page 9 and crewel needle, embroider flowers using stem stitch (see Glossary, page 133) in center of each stepped diamond as shown on diagram, backing each flower with a 3" (7.5-cm) circle of muslin on the WS of yoke. If desired, embroider partial flowers in partial stepped diamonds along edges as shown, backing each partial flower as for full flowers. When each flower is completed, trim muslin close to stitching on WS. Carefully cut open a buttonhole in right front yoke about 1¼" (3.2 cm) away from point. With MC on a tapestry needle, finish buttonhole by working buttonhole stitch (see Glossary, page 133) around the buttonhole opening.

Body

Right Half

With waste yarn and ribbon, and using the ribbon method provisional cast-on (see Glossary, page 131), CO 96 sts. Change to single strand of MC. Working in garter st, inc 1 st at end of RS rows (see Stitch Guide) every 6th row 6 times, then every 4th row 26 times—128 sts; 140 rows completed; piece measures about 15½" (39.5 cm) from CO. Inc 1 st at end of next 73 RS rows, ending with a WS row—201 sts; piece measures about 31¾" (80.5 cm) from CO. Cont to inc at end of RS rows while working short-rows (see Glossary, page 136) as foll:

Row 1: (RS) Inc 1 st at end of row—202 sts.

Row 2: Knit to last 10 sts, wrap next st, turn.

Row 3: Knit to end, inc 1 st at end of row—1 st inc'd.

Row 4: Knit to 10 sts before previous wrapped st, wrap next st, turn.

Rows 5–38: Rep Rows 3 and 4 seventeen more times—220 sts total on needle; 19 wrapped sts;

Embroidery Diagram

center back yoke

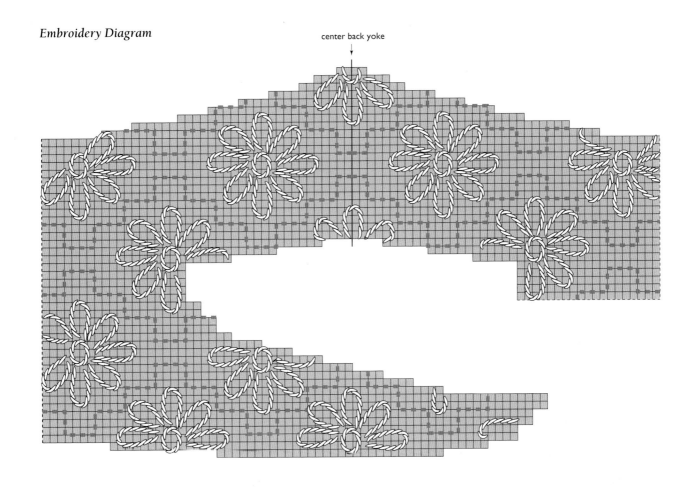

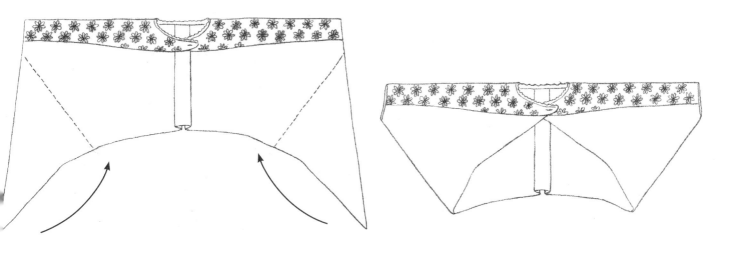

last wrapped st is 31st st from end of row when RS is facing.

Row 39: Knit to end without increasing.

Row 40: Knit to 10 sts before previous wrapped st, wrap next st, turn.

Rows 41 and 42: Rep Rows 39 and 40 once more—still 220 sts total; 21 wrapped sts, last wrapped st is 11th st from end of row when RS is facing.

Knit 4 rows, working wrapped sts tog with their wraps when you come to them on the first row—220 sts; piece measures about 32½" (82.5 cm) from CO, measured straight up along shorter selvedge at beg of RS rows. BO all sts very loosely, using a spare larger size needle if necessary.

Left Half

Carefully remove waste yarn and ribbon from base of provisional CO of right half and place 96 sts on needle. Rejoin single strand of MC with RS facing. Working in garter st, inc 1 st at beg of RS rows (see Stitch Guide) every 6 rows 6 times, then every 4 rows 26 times—128 sts; 140 rows completed; piece measures about 15½" (39.5 cm) from CO. Inc 1 st at beg of next 73 RS rows, ending with a WS row—201 sts; piece measures about 31¾" (80.5 cm) from CO. Cont to inc at beg of RS rows while working short-rows as foll:

Row 1: (RS) Inc 1 st at beg of row, knit to last 10 sts, wrap next st, turn—202 sts.

Row 2: Knit to end.

Row 3: Inc 1 st at beg of row, knit to 10 sts before previous wrapped st, wrap next st, turn—1 st inc'd.

Row 4: Knit to end.

Rows 5–38: Rep Rows 3 and 4 seventeen more times—220 sts total on needle; 19 wrapped sts; last wrapped st is 31st st from beg of row when RS is facing.

Row 39: *Without* inc at beg of row, knit to 10 sts before previous wrapped st, wrap next st, turn.

Row 40: Knit to end.

Rows 41 and 42: Rep Rows 39 and 40 once more—still 220 sts total; 21 wrapped sts, last wrapped st is 11th st from beg of row when RS is facing.

Knit 4 rows, working wrapped sts tog with their wraps when you come to them on the first row—220 sts; piece measures about 32½" (82.5 cm) from CO, measured straight up along shorter selvedge at end of RS rows. BO all sts very loosely, using a spare larger size needle if necessary.

Finishing

Prepare Lining

Using the yoke as a template, cut yoke lining from lining material, allowing a ½" (1.3-cm) seam allowance on all sides. Turn under seam allowance of lining ½" (1.3 cm) to WS on all sides and finger-press in place. Set yoke lining aside.

Upper Back Seam

The shorter, unshaped selvedges of the right and left half are the upper back edge of the body. Pin the center of this edge (where the two halves are joined) to the center of the lower back edge of the yoke. Pin each end of the same body edge to the ends of the back yoke. Pin the rest of the body edge to the yoke, working from the ends of the yoke toward the center. Because the back edge of the yoke is about 60" (152.5 cm) wide and the upper back edge of the body is about 65" (165 cm) wide, you will have some excess body fabric. Fold the excess fabric evenly on either side of the centerline to create a box pleat in the middle of the back. With MC threaded on a tapestry needle, use a backstitch seam (see Glossary,

page 136) to sew the body to the yoke in the "ditch" at the base of the yoke's crochet edging, sewing through all layers of the pleat; the yoke edging should remain free and slightly overlap the body.

Upper Front Seams

Lay the wrap flat with the yoke folded lengthwise along the shoulder line and the front yokes facing you. The sloped, bound-off edges of the body will be sewn to the lower front edges of the yoke. Fold the pointed end of the right body half up to meet the pointed end of the right front yoke. Pin the bound-off edge of the body to the front yoke, working from the center outwards. Because the bound-off edge of the body is wider than the lower edge of the front yoke, the remaining few inches of the body edge will be left unattached, leaving a hand opening at the end of the "sleeve." With MC threaded on a tapestry needle and using a backstitch seam, sew the body to the front yoke in the "ditch" at the base of the yoke's crochet edging as for the back. Fold the pointed end of the left body half up to meet the pointed end of the

left front yoke, and sew in place as for the right front, making sure that the two sleeve openings are the same size.

Weave in loose ends. Wash in cold water with mild soap or shampoo and rinse with hair conditioner. Lay flat to dry. When slightly damp, lightly steam-block on WS.

Attach Lining

With sewing needle and thread, slip-stitch (see Glossary, page 136) lining to WS of wrap to cover the inside of the yoke. *Carefully* cut a slit in the lining corresponding to the buttonhole of right front yoke. With sewing needle and thread, work buttonhole stitch around raw edge of lining slit, then sew invisibly around the edges of the buttonhole through all layers (yoke and lining). Sew button to end of left front yoke to correspond to buttonhole.

Crocheted Cloche

See Glossary, page 132, for crochet instructions.

Crown

With smaller crochet hook and double strand of MC, ch 4. Sl st

into first ch to form a ring. Work 6 sc in ring, and place removable marker (m) or safety pin in last sc to mark end of rnd. Repositioning the m in the last st of each rnd, work sc in the rnd in a spiral (do not join with a sl st at end of rnds) as foll:

Rnds 1 and 2: Work 2 sc in each sc around—12 sts after Rnd 1; 24 sts after Rnd 2.

Odd-numbered Rnds 3–19: Work 1 sc in each sc around.

Rnd 4: *Work 1 sc in next sc, work 2 sc in foll sc; rep from * to end—36 sts.

Rnd 6: *Work 1 sc in each of next

Color placement for embroidered flowers

Cuff

2 sc, work 2 sc in foll sc; rep from * to end—48 sts.

Rnd 8: *Work 1 sc in each of next 3 sc, work 2 sc in foll sc; rep from * to end—60 sts.

Rnd 10: *Work 1 sc in each of next 4 sc, work 2 sc in foll sc; rep from * to end—72 sts.

Rnd 12: *Work 1 sc in each of next 5 sc, work 2 sc in foll sc; rep from * to end—84 sts.

Rnd 14: *Work 1 sc in each of next 6 sc, work 2 sc in foll sc; rep from * to end—96 sts.

Rnd 16: *Work 1 sc in each of next 7 sc, work 2 sc in foll sc; rep from * to end—108 sts.

Rnd 18: *Work 1 sc in each of next 8 sc, work 2 sc in foll sc; rep from * to end—120 sts.

Rnd 20: *Work 1 sc in each of next 23 sc, work 2 sc in foll sc; rep from * to end—125 sts—crown measures about 6" (15 cm) across.

Lacy Crochet Pattern

(worked back and forth in rows)

Row 1: (RS) *Work [1 sc, ch 5, 3 tr] all in same sc, skip next 4 sc; rep from * to end, work 1 sc in sc at base of first ch-5 of row to join beg and end of row into a ring, turn.

Rows 2–6: Work 1 sc in top of each tr at end of previous row (3 sc total), *work [1 sc, ch 5, 3 tr] all in next ch-5 space; rep from * to end, work 1 sc in sc in first sc at beg of row to join beg and end of row into a ring, turn.

When Row 6 of lacy patt has been completed, resume working in the rnd with RS facing as foll, re-positioning removable m at end of each rnd as before. *Next rnd:* (RS) *Work 1 hdc in first tr, 1 sc in each of next 2 tr, 1 sc in top of ch-5, 1 dc in sc; rep from * to end, mark last st with removable m for end of rnd. Next rnd: Work 1 sc in each st of previous rnd—125 sts. Work 8 rnds even in sc—10 rnds total completed from end of lacy crochet patt.

Brim

Change to larger crochet hook. Shape brim as foll:

Rnd 1: *Work 1 sc in each of next 4 sc, work 2 sc in foll sc; rep from * to end—150 sts.

Rnd 2: *Work 1 sc in each of next 5 sc, work 2 sc in foll sc; rep from * to end—175 sts.

Rnd 3: *Work 1 sc in each of next 6 sc, work 2 sc in foll sc; rep from * to end—200 sts.

Rnd 4: *Work 1 sc in each of next 19 sc, work 2 sc in foll sc; rep from * to end—210 sts. Work 5 rnds even in sc. Work 1 rnd reverse sc. Fasten off.

Flowers

Center Bud

(make 1 each of lemon, gold, and light blue) With smaller crochet hook for cloche and perle cotton yarn doubled, ch 3. Sl st into first ch to form a ring. Work 6 sc in ring, and place removable m or safety pin in last sc to mark end of rnd. Repositioning the m in the last st of each rnd, cont as foll:

Rnd 1: Work 2 sc in each sc around—12 sts.

Rnds 2 and 3: Work 1 sc in each sc around.

Rnd 4: *Work 1 sc in next sc, skip foll sc; rep from * around—6 sts.

Small Petals

Change to petal color, using magenta with light blue bud, peri-winkle with gold bud, and lime with yellow bud, and cont working petals back and forth in rows as foll:

Row 1: Work 1 sc in next sc of center bud, ch 3, skip 1 sc, work 1 sc in next sc, ch 2, turn.

Row 2: Work 4 hdc all in ch-3 loop, ch 2, turn;

Rows 3 and 4: Work 1 hdc in each hdc of previous row, ch 2, turn.

First small petal ends with WS facing. Secure end of petal to center bud by working 1 sc in next sc of center bud (counts as first sc of Row 1 for second small petal), then rep Rows 1–4 for second small petal, beg with WS facing, and end by working Row 4 with RS facing. Secure end of petal to center bud by working 1 sc in next sc of center bud (counts as first sc of Row 1 for third small petal), then rep Rows 1–4 for third small petal, working Row 1 with RS facing, and working the second sc of Row 1 in the skipped sc of the second small petal. Third small petal ends with WS facing. Secure end of third small petal to center bud by working 1 sc in next sc (counts as first sc of first medium petal). Do not cut yarn.

Medium Petals

Cont to work medium petals behind small petals as foll:

Row 1: Work 1 sc in next sc, ch 4, skip 1 sc, work 1 sc in back of next sc of center bud, ch 2, turn.

Row 2: Work 8 hdc all in ch-4 loop, ch 2, turn;

Rows 3 and 4: Work 1 hdc in each hdc of previous row, ch 2, turn.

First medium petal ends with RS facing. Secure end of petal to center bud by working 1 sc in back next sc of center bud (counts as first sc of Row 1 for next medium petal), then rep Rows 1–4 for next medium petal, and end by working Row 4 with RS facing. Secure end of petal to center bud by working 1 sc in next sc of center bud (counts as first sc of foll petal). Cont in this manner until you have worked a total of 2 to 4 medium petals, as desired. Fasten off last st.

Finishing

Weave in loose ends. Wash and block as for wrap. With MC threaded on a tapestry needle, sew flowers in place as desired.

Short Asymmetrical Jacket and Flower Pin

T he geometric embroidered pattern for this short jacket came from a piece of embroidered tapestry from the Nazca era. The tapestry was further embellished with flowers, but I liked the serpentine embroidery so much by itself that I decided to leave it alone. This jacket has unusual asymmetrical fronts that drape open beautifully or that may be fastened with a brooch—or knitted flower pin! A high collar and narrow sleeves that can be pushed up the arm give the jacket a sophisticated look.

Finished Size Jacket: 35½ (40, 46½)" (87.5 [101.5, 118] cm) bust circumference, closed. *Note:* Jacket may be left open or front overlap can be adjusted for a roomier fit, to produce a slightly larger size when worn. Flower pin: About 3" (7.5 cm) across.

Yarn CYCA #3 Light (DK weight). *Shown here:* The Alpaca Yarn Company Classic Alpaca (100% superfine alpaca; 110 yd [100 m]/50 g): #2201 sweet potato (orange, MC), 14 (15, 17) skeins; #1660 Annapolis navy (CC), 2 skeins (includes enough for flower pin). Flower pin alone takes about 40 yd (36 m).

Needles Jacket body and sleeves— size 6 (4 mm): 32" (80 cm) circular (cir). Jacket facings and collar—size 5 (3.75 mm): 32" (80 cm) cir, and spare

cir or straight needle in same size. Flower pin—size 8 (5 mm): straight. Adjust needle size if necessary to obtain the correct gauge.

Notions A few yards (meters) of waste yarn and smooth, satin ribbon for provisional cast-on; markers (m); tapestry needle; stitch holders; 1" (2.5 cm) pin backing for flower (available from craft, bead, or jewelry suppliers).

Gauge 20 sts and 29 rows = 4" (10 cm) in St st on larger needles for jacket. Exact gauge for flower pin is not critical.

Notes

• This garment is planned to have a fixed number of rows for the body and sleeves to accommodate the

embroidery as shown; all pieces are the same length for all sizes.
• The finished "wingspan" of the jacket is planned to be 60½" (153.5 cm) from cuff to cuff for all sizes. To customize sleeve length, cast on more or fewer stitches in the final cast-on row for each sleeve; every 5 stitches added or subtracted will lengthen or shorten the sleeve by about 1" (2.5 cm). Make a note of any changes so you can work sleeve shaping to match on all pieces.
• Because the larger sizes have increasingly wider bodies, they have correspondingly shorter sleeves in order to keep the wingspan identical for all sizes.

Back and Back Sleeves

Lower Back

With larger needle for jacket, waste yarn and ribbon, and using the ribbon method provisional cast-on (see Glossary, page 131), CO 86 (100, 116) sts. Change to MC. Work even in St st for 52 rows, ending with a WS row— piece should measure about 7¼" (18.5 cm) from CO.

Shape Sleeves

See Notes (page 13) for customizing sleeve length. Using the cable method (see Glossary, page 131), CO 7 (7, 6) sts at beg of next 24 (20, 20) rows, then CO 4 sts at beg of next 6 (10, 10) rows, then CO 12 (11, 13) sts at beg of next 2 rows—302 sts for all sizes; 32 rows in sleeve shaping; piece measures about 11½" (29 cm) from CO. Work even in St st for 36 more rows, ending with a WS row—120 St st rows completed;

piece measures about 16½" (42 cm) from CO; armholes measure about 9¼" (23.5 cm). Place center 36 (42, 48) sts on holder for back neck, then place rem 133 (130, 127) sts at each side on separate holders or lengths of waste yarn.

Left Sleeve and Front

With larger needle for jacket, waste yarn and ribbon, and using the ribbon method provisional cast-on, CO 52 (61, 71) sts. Change to MC. Work 2 rows even in St st, ending with a WS row.

Shape Left Front

Beg with the next RS row, [inc 1 st at center front edge (end of RS rows) on next RS row, work 5 rows even] 8 times—60 (69, 79) sts. Inc 1 st at center front edge on next RS row, then work 1 WS row even—52 rows completed; piece measures about 7¼" (18.5 cm)

from CO. *Note:* Lapel shaping continues at same time as sleeve shaping is introduced; please read the next sections all the way through before proceeding. At front edge, work 4 rows even, [inc 1 st at center front edge on next RS row, work 5 rows even] 7 times, work 2 more rows even, ending with a WS row—16 sts total inc'd at neck edge; 100 rows completed; piece measures about 13¾" (35 cm) from lower edge CO at end of left front shaping. *At the same time,* beg with the 53rd row, shape left sleeve as foll:

Shape Left Sleeve

(RS; Row 53) Using the cable method, CO 7 (7, 6) sts at beg of next 12 (10, 10) RS rows, then CO 4 sts at beg of next 3 (5, 5) RS rows, then CO 12 (11, 13) sts at beg of next RS row—108 (101, 93) sts total CO for sleeve. When all left front and sleeve shaping have

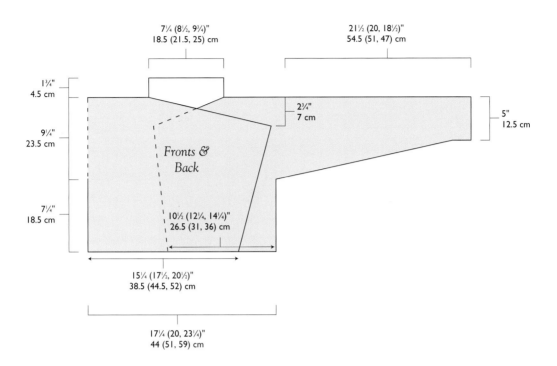

7¼ (8½, 9¾)"
18.5 (21.5, 25) cm

21½ (20, 18½)"
54.5 (51, 47) cm

1¾"
4.5 cm

2¾"
7 cm

5"
12.5 cm

9¼"
23.5 cm

Fronts &
Back

7¼"
18.5 cm

10½ (12¼, 14¼)"
26.5 (31, 36) cm

15¼ (17½, 20½)"
38.5 (44.5, 52) cm

17¼ (20, 23¼)"
44 (51, 59) cm

been completed there will be 176 (178, 180) sts.

Shape Front Neck

Beg with next WS row (102nd row from CO), at neck edge (beg of WS rows) BO 3 sts 4 (6, 8) times, then BO 2 sts 5 (3, 1) time(s)—154 sts rem for all sizes. Work even until 120 rows has been completed from CO; piece measures about 16½" (42 cm) from beg. Place 21 (24, 27) sts at neck edge on holder for left front neck, then place rem 133 (130, 127) sleeve sts on separate holder or length of waste yarn.

Right Sleeve and Front

With larger needle for jacket, waste yarn and ribbon, and using the ribbon method provisional cast-on, CO 76 (88, 102) sts. Change to MC. Work 2 rows even in St st, ending with a WS row.

Shape Right Front

Beg with the next RS row, [inc 1 st at center front edge (beg of RS rows) on next RS row, work 5 rows even] 8 times—84 (96, 110) sts. Inc 1 st at center front edge on next RS row, then work 1 WS row even—52 rows completed; piece measures about 7¼" (18.5 cm) from CO. *Note:* Lapel shaping continues at same time as sleeve shaping is introduced; read the next sections all the way through before proceeding. At front edge, work 4 rows even, [inc 1 st at center front edge on next RS row, work 5 rows even] 7 times, work 2 more rows even, ending with a WS row—16 sts total inc'd at neck edge; 100 rows completed; piece measures about 13¾" (35 cm) from lower edge CO at end of right front shaping. *At the same time,* beg with the 54th row, shape right sleeve as foll:

Shape Right Sleeve

(WS; Row 54) Use the cable method to CO 7 (7, 6) sts at beg of next 12 (10, 10) WS rows, then CO 4 sts at beg of next 3 (5, 5) WS rows, then CO 12 (11, 13) sts at beg of next WS row—108 (101, 93) sts total CO for sleeve. When all neck and sleeve shaping have been completed there will be 200 (205, 211) sts.

Shape front neck

Beg with next RS row (Row 101), BO at neck edge (beg of RS rows) 7 sts 0 (1, 3) time(s), then 6 sts 1 (4, 6) time(s), then 5 sts 8 (4, 0) times—154 sts rem for all sizes. Work even until 120 rows have been completed from lower edge CO; piece measures about 16½" (42 cm) from beg. Place 21 (24, 27) sts at neck edge on holder for right front neck, then place rem 133 (130, 127) sleeve sts on separate holder or length of scrap yarn.

Join Fronts and Back

With MC threaded on a tapestry needle, RS facing, and beg at cuffs and working toward neck opening, graft live sts of fronts and backs tog at shoulders (see Glossary, page 134).

Lower Back and Cuff Facings

Lower Back

Carefully remove waste yarn and ribbon from provisional CO at lower back, and place 86 (100, 116) live sts on smaller cir needle for jacket. Join MC with RS facing, and knit 1 RS row. Knit the next WS row for fold line. Work even in St st for 10 rows, ending with a WS row. BO all sts.

Cuffs

With MC, smaller cir needle for jacket, and RS facing, pick up and knit 50 sts along selvedge of cuff. Knit the next WS row for fold line. Work even in St st for 10 rows, ending with a WS row. BO all sts.

Right Front Facing

Carefully remove waste yarn and ribbon from provisional CO and place 76 (88, 102) live sts on smaller cir needle for jacket. Join MC with RS facing. K76 (88, 102) sts of lower right front edge, place marker (pm), then pick up and knit 100 sts along diagonal edge of right front lapel (1 st for every row), then pick up and knit

46 (51, 57) sts along BO edge of neck shaping—222 (239, 259) sts total. Knit the next WS row for fold line, then knit 1 RS row. *Next row:* (WS) P46 (51, 57), [p2tog *very* loosely] 50 times to reduce the 100 sts picked-up along center front opening to 50 sts, p76 (88, 102) sts—172 (189, 209) sts rem. Cont in short-rows, joining facing sts to sts along center front edge as foll:

Row 1: (RS) K75 (87, 101) to last st of lower edge, slip next st as if to knit (sl 1 kwise), temporarily remove marker (m), k1 from center front edge, pass the slipped st over (psso), replace m, turn—1 st joined from center front edge.

Rows 2, 4, 6, 8, and 10: Purl to end.

Row 3: K73 (85, 99) to last 3 sts of lower edge, k1f&b (see Glossary, page 135), k1, sl 1 kwise, remove m, k1 from center front edge, psso, replace m, turn—1 st inc'd for lapel shaping; 1 st joined from center front edge.

Rows 5 and 7: Knit to 1 st before m, sl 1 kwise, remove m, k1 from center front edge, psso, replace m, turn.

Row 9: Knit to 3 sts before m, k1f&b, k1, sl 1 kwise, remove m, k1 from center front edge, psso, replace m, turn—1 st inc'd for lapel shaping; 1 st joined from center front edge.

Row 11: BO 25 (29, 34) sts, knit to 1 st before m, sl 1 kwise, remove m, k1 from center front edge, psso, replace m, turn—53

(61, 70) sts rem before m; 1 st joined from center front edge.

Rows 12, 14, 16, 18, and 20: Purl to end.

Row 13: Knit to 1 st before m, sl 1 kwise, remove m, k1 from center front edge, psso, replace m, turn—1 st joined from center front edge.

Row 15: Knit to 3 sts before m, k1f&b, k1, sl 1 kwise, remove m, k1 from center front edge, psso, replace m, turn—1 st inc'd for lapel shaping; 1 st joined from center front edge.

Rows 17 and 19: Rep Row 13.

Row 21: Rep Row 15.

Row 22: Purl to end.

Rows 23–94: Rep Rows 17–22 twelve more times—67 (75, 84) sts before m with RS facing; 16 sts total inc'd for lapel shaping; 47 sts total joined from center front edge at end of RS rows.

Rows 95, 97, and 99: Rep Row 13.

Rows 96, 98, and 100: Purl to end—all 50 center front edge sts have been joined; 113 (126, 141) sts total on needle; with RS facing, 67 (75, 84) sts before m, and 46 (51, 57) sts after m from pick-up along the BO edge of neck shaping.

Shape top edge of facing to match BO neck edge of right front using short-rows as foll:

Row 1: (RS) K61 (68, 77) to 6 (7, 7) sts before m, wrap next st (see Glossary, page 136), turn.

Even-numbered Rows 2–16: Purl to end.

Rows 3 and 5: Knit to 5 (6, 7) sts before previous wrapped st, wrap next st, turn.

Rows 7 and 9: Knit to 5 (6, 6) sts before previous wrapped st, wrap next st, turn.

Rows 11, 13, 15, and 17: Knit to 5 (5, 6) sts before previous wrapped st, wrap next st, turn.

Row 18: Purl to end.

On the next RS row, k67 (75, 84), working wrapped sts tog with their wraps as you come to them; you should be at the marker. Break yarn and remove marker. With RS facing, place first 21 (24, 27) sts on holder to be worked later as part of collar. Divide rem 92 (102, 114) sts evenly on 2 needles with wrong sides touching—46 (51, 57) sts on each needle. With MC threaded on a tapestry needle and RS facing, use the Kitchener st to join the sts at shaped top edge of right lapel. With MC threaded on a tapestry needle, work a line of backstitches (see Glossary, page 133) through both layers very close to the purled fold line along the shaped top edge of right lapel and down the center front edge to secure facing in place.

Left Front Facing

With smaller cir needle for jacket and RS facing, pick up and knit 22 (24, 26) sts along BO edge of neck shaping, then pick up and knit 100 sts along diagonal edge of left front lapel (1 st for every row), pm, carefully remove waste yarn and ribbon from provisional CO and place 52 (61, 71) live sts on left needle, knit across lower

edge sts to end—174 (185, 197) sts total. Knit the next WS row for fold line. *Next row:* (RS) K22 (24, 26), [p2tog *very* loosely] 50 times to reduce the 100 sts picked-up along center front opening to 50 sts, k52 (61, 71)—124 (135, 147) sts. Cont in short-rows, joining facing sts to sts along center front as foll:

Row 1: (WS) P51 (60, 70) to last st of lower edge, sl next st as if to purl (sl 1 pwise), remove m, return slipped st to left needle, p2tog (last st of lower edge tog with 1 st from center front edge), replace m, turn—1 st joined from center front edge.

Rows 2, 4, 6, 8, and 10: (RS) Knit to end.

Row 3: P49 (58, 68) to last 3 sts

of lower edge, p1f&b (see Glossary, page 135), p1, sl 1 pwise, remove m, return slipped st to left needle, p2tog, replace m, turn—1 st inc'd for lapel shaping; 1 st joined from center front edge.

Rows 5 and 7: Purl to 1 st before m, sl 1 pwise, remove m, return slipped st to left needle, p2tog, replace m, turn.

Row 9: Knit to 3 sts before m, p1f&b, p1, sl 1 pwise, remove m, return slipped st to left needle, p2tog, replace m, turn—1 st inc'd for lapel shaping; 1 st joined from center front edge.

Row 11: BO 25 (29, 34) sts, purl to 1 st before m, sl 1 pwise, remove m, return slipped st to left needle, p2tog, replace m, turn—29 (34, 39) sts rem before m; 1 st joined from center front edge.

Rows 12, 14, 16, 18, and 20: Knit to end.

Row 13: Purl to 1 st before m, sl 1 pwise, remove m, return slipped st to left needle, p2tog, replace m, turn—1 st joined from center front edge.

Row 15: Purl to 3 sts before m, p1f&b, p1, sl 1 pwise, remove m, return slipped st to left needle, p2tog, replace m, turn—1 st inc'd for lapel shaping; 1 st joined from center front edge.

Rows 17 and 19: Rep Row 13.

Row 21: Rep Row 15.

Row 22: Knit to end.

Rows 23–94: Rep Rows 17–22 twelve more times—43 (48, 53)

sts before m with WS facing; 16 sts total inc'd for lapel shaping; 47 sts total joined from center front edge at end of WS rows.

Rows 95, 97, and 99: Rep Row 13.

Rows 96, 98, and 100: Knit to end—all 50 center front edge sts have been joined; 65 (72, 79) sts total on needle; 43 (48, 53) sts before m with WS facing, and 22 (24, 26) sts after m from pick-up along the BO edge of neck shaping.

Shape top edge of facing to match BO neck edge using short-rows as foll:

Row 1: (WS) Purl to 3 sts before m, wrap next st, turn.

Even-numbered Rows 2–16: (RS) Knit to end.

Rows 3, 5, and 7: Purl to 3 sts before m, wrap next st, turn.

Rows 9 and 11: Purl to 2 (3, 3) sts before previous wrapped st, wrap next st, turn.

Rows 13 and 15: Purl to 2 (2, 3) sts before previous wrapped st, wrap next st, turn.

Row 17: Purl to 2 sts before previous wrapped st, wrap next st, turn.

Row 18: Knit to end.

On the next WS row, p43 (48, 53), working wrapped sts tog with their wraps as you come to them; you should be at the marker. Break yarn and remove marker. With RS facing, place last 21 (24, 27) sts on holder to be worked later for collar. Divide rem 44 (48, 52) sts evenly on 2 needles with

wrong sides touching—22 (24, 26) sts on each needle. With MC threaded on a tapestry needle and RS facing, use the Kitchener st to join the sts at shaped top edge of left lapel. With MC threaded on a tapestry needle, work a line of backstitches through both layers very close to the purled fold line along the shaped top edge of left lapel, and down the center front edge to secure facing in place.

Embroidery

Note: The embroidery patt is deliberately off-center and not symmetrical on either side of the back centerline. With CC threaded on a tapestry needle and beg in the center of back (indicated by heavy gridline on diagram) and working outward toward the back selvedges, work single lines of backstitch embroidery (see Glossary, page 133) according to diagram on page 19; do not work embroidery on the lower back facing. When you have reached the body selvedges of the back, continue the embroidery pattern along the sleeves to pick-up row for the cuff facings; do not work embroidery on cuff facings. For the 120 knitted rows of the body, you will work the 48 rows of the diagram 2½ times. With CC, embroider a line of backstitch along the entire shoulder line, from cuff to cuff, to finish off the top of the highest embroidery motifs. For left front, beg at selvedge of left side and working toward the front opening, work backstitch embroidery as a mirror image of the back; in other words, if the left front and back were placed tog with wrong sides touching, the left front embroidery would lie directly on top of the back embroidery. Work embroidery for right front in the same manner, working from selvedge at right side and mirroring the back embroidery. When you reach the column of sts on each front that corresponds to the center back, cont the embroidery in patt to the center front edge. For the front facings, work embroidery exactly aligned with the embroidered lines of the fronts themselves; in other words, even though you are embroidering the fronts and facings separately, the final effect should look as if the embroidery had been worked through both layers of each front and its facing at the same time.

Collar and Back Neck Facing

Collar

Place sts for fronts and back on smaller cir for jacket with RS facing in the foll order: 21 (24, 27) held right front sts, 36 (42, 48) held back sts, 21 (24, 27) held left front sts—78 (90, 102) sts total. Join MC with RS facing and knit 1 RS row. *Next row:* (WS) Place 21 (24, 27) held sts of left front facing on spare needle and hold in front of work. *Insert right needle tip into first st on facing and body needles, k2tog (1 st from each needle tog)*, rep from * to * a total of 21 (24, 27) times to join all sts of left facing, k36 (42, 48) back neck sts, place 21 (24, 27) held sts of right front facing on spare needle and hold in front, rep from * to * a total of 21 (24, 27) times to join all sts of right facing—still 78 (90, 102) sts. Work even in St st for 11 rows for outside of collar, ending with a RS row. Knit 1 WS row for fold line. Work even

Embroidery Diagram

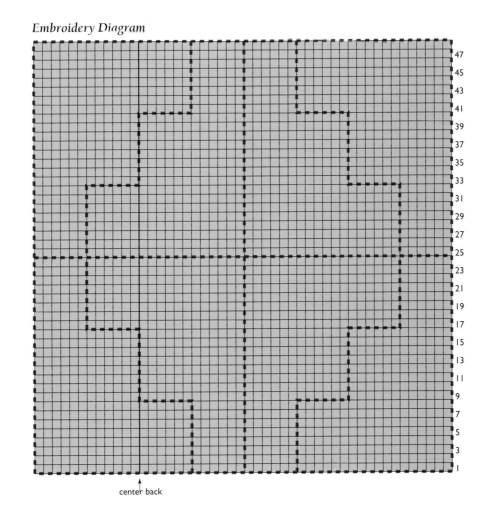

47
45
43
41
39
37
35
33
31
29
27
25
23
21
19
17
15
13
11
9
7
5
3
1

center back

in St st for 12 more rows for inside of collar, ending with a WS row. BO all sts. If desired, work vertical lines of backstitch embroidery on inside of collar, continuing stitching lines from body. Fold collar in half along fold line, and with MC threaded on a tapestry needle, sew short seams at each end of collar, leaving BO edge free.

Back Neck Facing

Mark center 44 (50, 56) sts of collar BO edge. With RS facing and smaller cir needle for jacket, pick up and knit 1 st for each BO st between markers—44 (50, 56) sts. *Next row:* (WS) P3, pm, p1, pm, p36 (42, 48), pm, p1, pm, p3.

Row 1: (RS) *Knit to 1 st before m, k1f&b, sl m, k1, sl m, k1f&b; rep from * once more, knit to end—4 sts inc'd.

Row 2: *Purl to 1 st before m, p1f&b, sl m, p1, sl m, p1f&b; rep from * once more, purl to end—4 sts inc'd.

Rows 3–8: Rep Rows 1 and 2 three more times—76 (82, 88) sts. BO all sts. With MC threaded on a tapestry needle, work a line of backstitches through both collar layers very close to the purled fold line at the base of the collar.

Finishing

With MC threaded on a tapestry needle, sew sleeve and side seams, including facings. Turn up cuff and lower facings along fold lines and slip-stitch (see Glossary, page 136) invisibly in place. Sew short selvedges of back neck facing to front facings where they meet. Slip-stitch straight selvedge of right front facing, back neck facing, and straight selvedge of left front facing invisibly in place on WS. Weave in loose ends. Wash in cold water with mild soap or shampoo and rinse with hair conditioner. Lay flat to dry. When slightly damp, lightly steam-block on WS.

Flower Pin

With CC, size 8 (5 mm) needles, and using the long-tail method (see Glossary, page 131), CO 12 sts. Work even in St st until piece measures about 20" (51 cm) from CO. BO all sts. Fold the knitted strip in half lengthwise and coil it around itself to form a spiral, sewing layers of the spiral in place with yarn threaded on a tapestry needle as you go. Gather the strip in some places, and stretch it in others randomly to produce a slightly irregular effect. With CC threaded on a tapestry needle, sew pin backing to WS of flower. Weave in loose ends.

Peruvian Textiles

Textiles represent an important part of Peruvian history. Necessary for warmth and protection in the harsh environment, they were also used to record events, as a form of currency, an indication of status and wealth, and as an important part of religious ceremonies. Elaborate textiles, the oldest evidence of pre-Columbian art, were woven long before gold was hammered into jewelry and clay manipulated into vessels. Made on the primitive backstrap loom, the fabric is nonetheless finer than modern cloth.

The earliest textiles were simple cords, nets, mats, and baskets, made from twisted and braided vegetable fibers such as rushes, cattail, and maguey. Woven fabrics date back to about 2000 B.C., around the same time that cotton was first cultivated along the coastal regions and alpacas and their relatives were domesticated in the highlands. Due to the dry desert conditions of coastal Peru, thousands of these textiles have survived in excellent shape.

Each piece of fabric resulted from the efforts of many people with diverse talents. Herdsmen bred animals for the finest, whitest fiber, and farmers cultivated the softest, whitest cotton. Using a limited range of indigenous plants and insects, dyers transformed the white fiber into a variety of rich, long-lasting colors. Spinners then worked the fiber into fine threads of unequalled consistency. Weavers, many of them skilled designers, interlaced the threads into intricate patterns to form cloth. Many of the textiles were further embellished with colorful detailed embroidery or printed patterns. By today's standards, these textiles represent remarkable craftsmanship, all the more noteworthy because of the primitive tools with which they were made—the fibers were spun on drop spindles and the fabrics were woven on simple backstrap looms.

Because they were so valued in pre-Columbian times, textiles were used as a type of regional currency and were distributed to needy families, disgruntled troops, and defeated provinces. In turn, the people were expected to surrender fabrics (particularly those made from alpaca) to the rulers and religious leaders as a form of tax or tribute.

Women were responsible for all aspects of textile production from spinning the fibers to weaving the fabrics. Many of the best weavers lived in tight-knit sanctuaries or communities, much like present-day convents, in which dozens to hundreds of women devoted their lives to producing exquisite textiles for nobility and religious ceremonies.

For the most part, villages in pre-Columbian Peru were isolated and travel between them limited. Consequently, each village developed its own combination of technique, color, and design so that weavings became a source of regional identification. As roads were constructed and the villages connected to one another, a traveler's origin could be revealed by the clothing he or she wore.

Long Asymmetrical Cardigan

For this cardigan, I combined design elements from tapestries of the Huari and Nazca cultures. Although they are distinctly different—the Huari tapestry features a multicolored geometrical stepped pattern and the Nazca features interlocking geometrical shapes—they complement each other beautifully. One side of the cardigan is worked in the stepped pattern, and for a touch of fun, the other side is worked in simple stripes of the same earthy tones. The cardigan has an asymmetrical silhouette, with the right front edge running along the diagonal from the lower right side to the left shoulder, and is held closed with a wooden button. An embroidered panel of Nazca geometric shapes embellishes the upper edge of the right front.

Finished Size 57" (145 cm) bust/chest circumference. *Note:* Front overlap can be adjusted by changing the button placement.

Yarn CYCA #3 Light (DK weight). *Shown here:* The Alpaca Yarn Company Classic Alpaca (100% superfine alpaca; 110 yd [100 m]/50 g): #2201 sweet potato (orange, MC), 6 skeins; #2213 cayenne (orange-red), #2406 butternut (gold), #2214 cider (orange-brown heather), #2023 flame (medium brown), #2211 mahogany (dark brown), and #0410 Oregon brown (brown-black), 3 skeins each.

CYCA #3 Light (DK). *Shown here:* Alpaca with a Twist Baby Twist (100% baby alpaca; 110 yd [100 m]/50 g): #5006 lemon zest (yellow) and #5003 autumn leaves (brown heather), 3 skeins each.

Needles Body and sleeves—size 6 (4 mm): 32" (80 cm) circular needle (cir). Facings—size 4 (3.5 mm): 32" (80 cm) cir. Adjust needle size if necessary to obtain the correct gauge.

Notions Markers (m); stitch holders; tapestry needle; small amount of waste yarn and smooth, satin ribbon for provisional cast-on; one 2½" (6.5 cm) button. Optional: one 3½ × 18" (9 × 45.5 cm) piece of 11-count Aida cloth; needlework marking pen; size 18 tapestry or crewel needle for embroidery; needlepoint frame.

Gauge 22 sts and 28 rows = 4" (10 cm) in St st using larger needles.

- The cardigan is worked in two halves, each knit from cuff to center, which are grafted together at center back.
- The color-work pattern for the left half is shown divided over three charts for readability: Left Sleeve,

Left Back, and Left Front. For the body, read across RS Row 1 of the Left Back chart, then read across RS Row 1 of the Left Front chart. After the left front has been completed, continue to work on the stitches of the Left Back chart only.

- The optional embroidered panel shown on the front right neckband is worked separately and sewn in place during finishing.

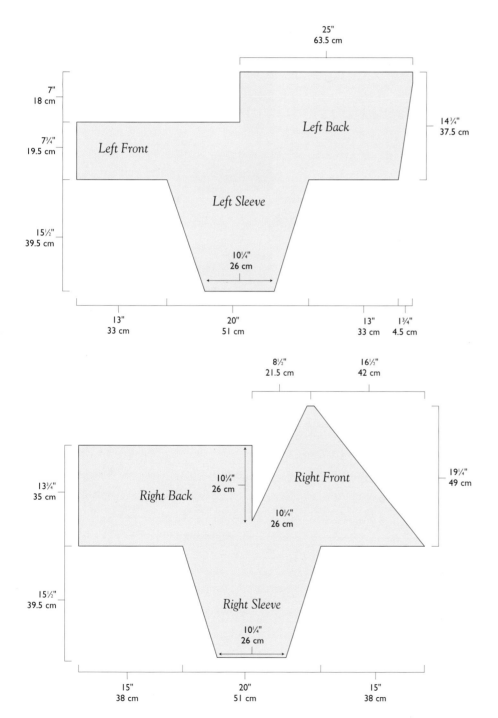

Right Sleeve

With smaller cir needle and orange, CO 56 sts. Do not join. Work St st back and forth in rows until piece measures 1½" (3.8 cm), ending with a RS row. Knit the next WS row for fold line. Change to larger cir needle. *Note:* Sleeve shaping is worked at same time as color changes for stripes; read the next section all the way through before proceeding.

Shape Sleeve

Work St st stripes in color order given below, and *at the same time,* beg with the first RS row inc 1 st at each end of needle every 4 rows 27 times as foll: (RS) K2, k1f&b (see Glossary, page 135), knit to last 3 sts, k1f&b, k2. *At the same time,* work 6-row St st stripes in the foll color order: orange, medium brown, yellow, orange-red, dark brown, brown heather, gold, brown-black, orange-red, orange, yellow, medium brown, dark brown, brown-black, brown heather, gold, orange, orange-red—110 sts when all shaping and stripes have been completed; 108 rows and eighteen 6-row stripes above fold

line; piece measures about 15½" (39.5 cm) from fold line. Cut yarn.

Right Back and Front

With waste yarn and ribbon, and using the ribbon method provisional cast-on (see Glossary, page 131), CO 82 sts for right front at beg of needle holding sleeve sts so that the first group of sts to be worked on the next RS row will be the newly CO sts—192 sts total. Join medium brown with RS facing, and knit across right front and sleeve sts. With waste yarn and ribbon, and using the ribbon method provisional cast-on, CO 82 sts for right back at end of sts for right front and sleeve. Slip

sts without working them back to left-hand needle and knit across 82 sts for right back—274 sts total. Work 5 more rows medium brown to complete a 6-row stripe, ending with a WS row. *Note:* Right front shaping is worked at same time as color changes for stripes; read the next section all the way through before proceeding. Work 6 rows each of dark brown, brown heather, and yellow, and *at the same time* dec 4 sts at right front edge during every 6-row stripe as foll: Work k2tog at beg of 1st and 3rd rows of stripe, then work k2tog twice at beg of 5th row of stripe—4 sts dec'd for stripe. When three 6-row stripes have been completed from beg of front

and back, 262 sts rem; 12 sts total dec'd at right front edge.

Right Back

Place first 125 sts for right front on holder—137 sts rem for back. Rejoin orange-red with RS facing. Cont on back sts, working 6 rows St st of each color in the foll order: orange-red, brown-black, orange, gold, dark brown, orange, brown heather, orange-red, medium brown, brown-black, yellow, dark brown—back measures about 13¾" (35 cm) from provisional CO. Cut yarn, and place back sts on holder or scrap yarn.

Right Front

Return 125 held sts for right front to large cir needle. Join orange-red with RS facing. Working in stripe colors in the order given below, cont to dec 4 sts in every 6-row stripe at right front edge (beg of RS rows) as established, and *at the same time* shape neck edge (end of RS rows) by dec 4 sts every 10 rows as foll: [Work to last 2 sts of row, k2tog, work 1 row even] 3 times, work to last 2 sts of next row, k2tog, work 3 rows even—4 sts dec'd in 10 rows. While shaping both the right front and neck edges as given above, work 6-row St st stripes in the foll color order: orange-red, brown-black, orange, gold, dark brown, orange, brown heather, orange-red, medium brown, brown-black, yellow, dark brown, gold, brown heather, orange, medium brown, brown-black, orange-red—9 sts rem; eighteen 6-row stripes and 108 rows completed from where back and front divided; 22 stripes and 132 rows total from provisional CO for front. Join dark brown. *Next row:* (RS) [K2tog] 2 times, k3, k2tog—6 sts rem. Purl 1 WS row *Next row:* (RS) [K2tog] 3 times—3 sts rem; front measures about 19¼" (49 cm) from provisional CO at tallest point. BO all sts.

Left Sleeve

With smaller cir needle and orange, CO 56 sts. Do not join. Work St st back and forth in rows until piece measures 1½" (3.8 cm), ending with a RS row. Knit the next WS row for fold line. Change to larger cir needle. Work

in patt from Left Sleeve chart, twisting yarns at color changes in the intarsia method (see Glossary, page 135) to prevent holes, and beg with Row 1 of chart, inc 1 st at each end of needle every 4th row 27 times as foll: (RS) K2, k1f&b, knit to last 3 sts, k1f&b, k2—110 sts when Row 108 has been completed; sleeve measures about 15½" (39.5 cm) from fold line.

Left Back and Front

With waste yarn and ribbon, and using the ribbon method provisional cast on, CO 72 sts for left back at beg of needle holding sleeve sts so that the first group of sts to be worked on the next RS row will be the newly CO sts. Join colors as needed with RS facing, and work in patt from Row 1 of Left Back chart to middle of sleeve sts, then work in patt from Row 1 of Left Front chart to end of sts on needle. With waste yarn and ribbon, and using the ribbon method provisional cast-on, CO 72 sts for left front at end of sts for left back and sleeve. Slip sts without working them back to left-hand needle and cont Row 1 of Left Front chart to end—254 sts total; 127 sts for each chart. Work even in patts until Row 54 has been completed, inc 1 st at lower edge of left back (beg of RS rows) every 10th row beg with Row 3 as shown on chart—260 sts; 133 back sts and 127 front sts; piece measures 7¾" (19.5 cm) from provisional

+	orange
◆	orange-red
·	gold
◇	orange-brown heather
−	medium brown
○	dark brown
■	brown-black
☐	yellow
◻	brown heather

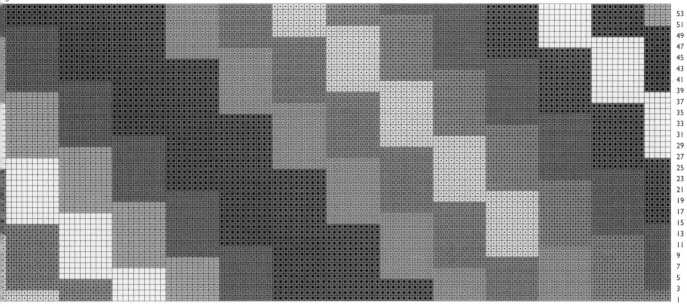

53
51
49
47
45
43
41
39
37
35
33
31
29
27
25
23
21
19
17
15
13
11
9
7
5
3
1

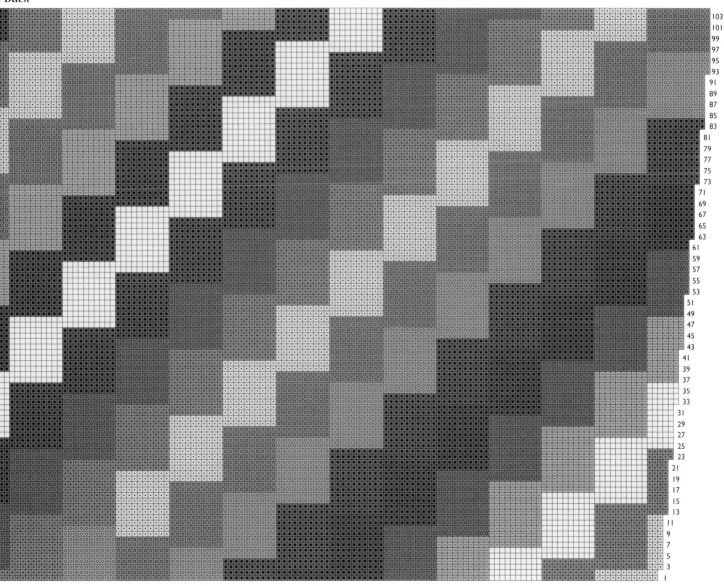

103
101
99
97
95
93
91
89
87
85
83
81
79
77
75
73
71
69
67
65
63
61
59
57
55
53
51
49
47
45
43
41
39
37
35
33
31
29
27
25
23
21
19
17
15
13
11
9
7
5
3
1

Left Sleeve

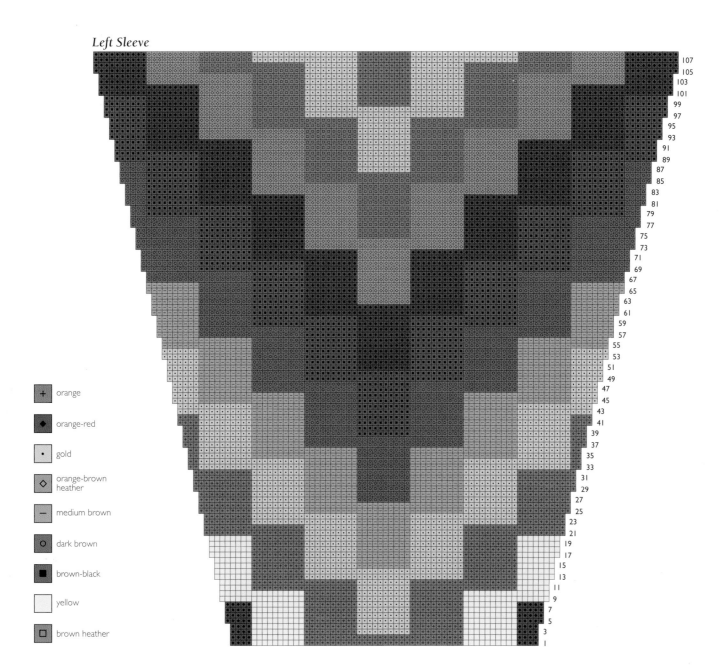

107
105
103
101
99
97
95
93
91
89
87
85
83
81
79
77
75
73
71
69
67
65
63
61
59
57
55
53
51
49
47
45
43
41
39
37
35
33
31
29
27
25
23
21
19
17
15
13
11
9
7
5
3
1

+ orange

◆ orange-red

• gold

◇ orange-brown heather

— medium brown

○ dark brown

■ brown-black

  yellow

□ brown heather

CO. Place 127 front sts on holder or waste yarn. Cont on back sts, inc as shown, until Row 104 of chart has been completed— 137 sts; back measures 14¾" (37.5 cm) from provisional CO. Place back sts on holder or waste yarn.

Join Right and Left Halves

With dark brown threaded on a tapestry needle, use the Kitchener st (see Glossary, page 134) to graft live sts from left and right backs tog. Graft left side seam, matching colors of intarsia pattern as much as possible. Graft right side seam using medium brown. Sew sleeve seams. Fold sleeve hems to WS along fold lines and slip-stitch (see Glossary, page 136) invisibly in place using orange threaded on a tapestry needle.

Right Front Neckband

With orange, smaller cir needle, and RS facing, pick up and knit 92 sts along neck edge of right front (2 sts from partial stripe at point and 5 sts along selvedge edge of each of 18 full stripes). Knit 1 WS row for decorative ridge. Work even in St st for 10 rows, ending with a WS row. *Buttonhole row:* (RS) K8, BO next 10 sts, knit to end. On the foll WS row, use the knitted method (see Glossary, page 131) to CO 10 sts over gap in previous row to complete buttonhole. Work 10 more rows in St st—22 rows completed from turning

ridge; neckband measures about 3¼" (8.5 cm) high. Purl 1 RS row for fold line. Work 10 rows even in St st, ending with a RS row. On the next WS row, purl to last 18 sts, BO 10 sts for buttonhole, purl to end. On the foll RS row, use the knitted method to CO 10 sts over gap in previous row to complete buttonhole. Work 10 more rows even in St st, ending with a RS row. BO all sts. If applying optional embroidered panel,

leave facing unfinished for now. If omitting embroidered panel, fold neckband along fold line, and using orange threaded on a tapestry needle, sew short side seams of neckband, then slipstitch lower edge of neckband invisibly in place on WS. With orange threaded on a tapestry needle, finish buttonhole by working buttonhole stitch (see Glossary, page 133) all around the buttonhole opening to join both layers.

Body Facing

With orange, smaller cir needle, RS facing, and beg at right back shoulder, pick up and knit 62 sts across back neck (about 1 st for every 2 rows), place marker (pm) for left shoulder corner. Return 127 held sts of left front to needle and knit across them, pm for lower left front corner. Pick up and knit 190 sts along lower edge to beg of right front shaping (about 3 sts for every 4 rows), pm for lower right front corner, pick up and knit 134 sts along diagonal edge of right front (6 sts for each full stripe and 2 sts from partial stripe at point)—513 sts total. Knit 1 WS row. *Mitered corner row:* (RS) Knit to left shoulder m, M1 (see Glossary, page 135), slip marker (sl m), M1, knit to 2 sts before lower left front corner m, ssk, sl m, k2tog, knit to right front corner m, sl m, ssk, knit to end—2 sts inc'd at left shoulder, 2 sts dec'd at left front corner, 1 st dec'd at right front corner; 1 st dec'd overall. Purl 1 WS row. Rep the last 2 rows 4 more times—508 sts; 10 St st rows completed; facing measures about 1¼" (3.2 cm). BO all sts loosely. Slipstitch facing invisibly in place on WS using orange threaded on a tapestry needle. If omitting embroidered panel, overlap shoulder end of right front neckband over back at shoulder line, and with orange threaded on a tapestry needle, sew short end of neckband and first few inches of neckband fold line to body, sewing through all layers (body and facing).

Embroidered Panel

Using a needlework marking pen, draw outline of motifs from Embroidery chart centered on the Aida cloth. Each square of the chart represents one square of the cloth. Secure cloth in needlepoint frame, and stitch the design from chart using mosaic stitch (see Glossary page 133), working from the top down. You may find it helpful to complete each color area before starting the next one. When embroidery is complete, steam or block if desired. Trim the fabric leaving a 1" (2.5 cm) border all the way around the embroidered area. Turn borders to WS along edge of embroidery and finger-press in place.

Embroidered Panel Border

With dark brown and smaller cir needle, CO 192 sts. Join for working in the rnd, being careful not to twist sts. Knit 8 rnds, then loosely BO all sts. With dark brown threaded on a tapestry needle and RS of embroidery facing, sew the CO edge of the border around all 4 sides of the embroidered panel so that the purl side of the border is the RS, stretching border to fit. Turn panel over, and slip-stitch BO edge of border to WS embroidered panel.

Attach Panel

Center embroidered panel on RS of right front neckband. With dark brown threaded on a tapestry needle, sew panel as invisibly as possible to outer layer of neckband—do not sew through both layers of neckband. Carefully cut open a buttonhole in embroidered panel to correspond with buttonhole of neckband. Fold neckband to WS along fold line, and using orange threaded on a tapestry needle, sew short side seams of neckband, then slipstitch lower edge of neckband invisibly in place on WS of garment. With orange threaded on a tapestry needle, finish buttonhole by working buttonhole stitch (see Glossary, page 133) around the buttonhole opening through all layers (embroidered panel and both layers of knitted neckband). Overlap shoulder end of finished neckband over back at shoulder line, and with orange threaded on a tapestry needle, sew short end of neckband and first few inches of neckband fold line to body, sewing through all layers (body and facing).

Finishing

Weave in loose ends. Wash in cold water with mild soap or shampoo and rinse with hair conditioner. Lay flat to dry. When slightly damp, lightly steam-block on WS. Try on cardigan to determine best location for button. Sew button in place securely.

ALPACAS THROUGH THE AGES

Much of the rich textile tradition in Peru can be attributed to the alpaca, which made its home in the Peruvian highlands centuries ago. Alpacas are ruminants and belong to the Camelidae family, which includes the camels and dromedaries of Asia and North Africa, as well as llamas, guanacos, and vicuñas of South America.

Surprisingly, although they are now identified with other continents, alpacas and their relatives originated in North America. Millions of years ago, ancestors of today's camelids called guanacos, which inhabited the prairies of North America, diverged into two migratory currents that underwent quite different anatomical, physiological, and behavioral developments. The group that traveled north, crossing the Bering Strait into Asia and Africa—where the arid climate forced them to adapt to long stretches without water, produced today's camels and dromedaries. The group that migrated south settled in the high altitudes of the central Andes and Patagonia and evolved into the wild guanaco, which can survive at high altitudes with little oxygen.

Although the intervention of early humans eventually drove out or killed any guanacos that remained in North America, early hunter-gatherers in the Andes domesticated large numbers of wild guanaco over thousands of years, eventually giving rise to two distinct animals—llamas and alpacas. Llamas, the larger of the two at about five feet tall and 300 pounds, have coarse hair and are primarily used as beasts of burden. Alpacas, the smaller animals that grow to about four feet tall and 160 pounds, were bred to provide rich, lustrous fiber. While domesticated guanaco gave rise to the llama and alpaca, some of the wild guanaco living at extreme elevations between 11,800 and 17,500 feet evolved naturally into the slender 110-pound vicuña. Because vicuñas have not been successfully domesticated, their exceptionally fine fiber remains relatively rare. Fiber from the wild guanaco is also uncommon. Throughout the world, there are many millions of llamas and alpacas, about 150,000 guanacos, and about 125,000 vicuñas.

During Incan times, herdsmen managed up to 1,000 animals each, and the alpaca played a pivotal role in the political, cultural, and financial development of the empire. The largest herds were owned by the state or religious center; smaller herds were owned by nobles or village communities. In a ceremony each spring, the herds were shorn separately and the coarser fibers were distributed among the commoners, while the finest fibers were reserved for nobility and ceremonial purposes.

Alpacas continue to be valued for their fiber, which rivals merino and cashmere in softness. These characteristics were recognized by some entrepreneurial individuals who, during the 1970s and 1980s, shipped some alpacas to different parts of the world, sometimes smuggling them across the southern border of Peru. Although there are now growing herds in the United States, Australia, New Zealand, Canada, Great Britain, and South Africa, the majority of the world's alpacas continue to live and thrive at the high elevations in the Andes.

Carlos Sala/PromPerú

Patchwork Kimono and Beaded Cap

Though stunning piece was inspired by a magnificent Huari tie-dyed tapestry that was woven more than a thousand years ago. Because the interlocking shapes and colors reminded me of some modern Japanese textiles, I decided to give the piece a kimono shape. The main fabric is knitted in the intarsia technique and smaller details are added with duplicate stitches and assorted beads. The kimono is worked in two halves, each consisting of a front, sleeve, and back. Fan-shaped inserts (shaped with short-rows) connect the two halves; the back fan is flared at the lower edge, the front fan is flared at the neck. The asymmetrical closure is fastened with a single stone button. The simple cap is knitted in the round in a rib pattern decorated with beads.

Finished Size Kimono: About 58" (147.5 cm) bust circumference. *Note:* Front overlap can be adjusted by changing the button placement to produce a smaller size when worn; for smaller figures, the ridged fabric of the center front and back panels can also be blocked into deeper pleats to make these pieces narrower. Cap: 19" (48.5 cm) circumference, will stretch up to 24" (61 cm).

Yarn CYCA Light (DK weight). *Shown here:* The Alpaca Yarn Company Classic Alpaca (100% superfine alpaca; 110 yd [100 m]/50 g). Kimono: #1411 green tea (MC, dark olive), 13 skeins; #2213 cayenne (orange-red),

#1810 purple mountain majesty, and #0410 Oregon brown, 3 skeins each; #2201 sweet potato (orange), 2 skeins. Cap: #1411 green tea, 2 skeins.

Needles Kimono patchwork intarsia—size 7 (4.5 mm): 32" (60 cm) circular (cir). Kimono center panels and hems—size 6 (4 mm): 20" (50 cm) and 32" (60 cm) cir. Cap body—size 6 (4 mm): straight. Cap ribbing—size 3 (3.25 mm): set of 4 or 5 double-pointed (dpn). Adjust needle size if necessary to obtain the correct gauge.

Notions A few yards (meters) of waste yarn and smooth, satin ribbon

for provisional cast-on for kimono and cap. For kimono: Stitch holders; tapestry needle; size C/2 (2.75 mm) crochet hook; assorted beads (shown here are: bronze pony, brown metal pony, size 8° iridescent purple cube, 4-mm orange round glass, and 10-mm orange glass lentil); one 1½" (3.8 cm) button; 8" (20.5 cm) of 1" (2.5 cm) grosgrain ribbon; 3 yd (2.75 m) coordinating lining fabric (optional); sharp-point sewing needle with eye small enough to fit through beads; sewing thread to match lining and bead colors; sewing pins. For cap: Removable markers (m); tapestry needle; beading needle (available at craft and bead shops); about 975 (25–30 g) size 8° seed beads in coordinating color.

Gauge Kimono: 20 sts and 28 rows = 4" (10 cm) in St st color-work patt from charts using larger needle for kimono. Cap: 19 sts and 33 rows = 4" (10 cm) in beaded patt st using larger needle for cap.

Stitch Guide

Place bead in stitch: With yarn in back, slide a bead along the working strand close to the needle, k1, pulling both new loop and bead through the old st, then adjust the position of the bead so that it lies on the RS of the fabric on the right-hand leg of the new st, oriented with the bead hole nearly vertical.

Place bead between stitches: With yarn in front, slide a bead along the working strand close to the needle, purl the next st, then adjust the position of the bead so that it lies on the RS of the fabric on the horizontal strand between the last two purl sts.

Notes

• The color-work sections are worked separately and connected by short-rowed panels that are worked from side to side.

• The color-work pattern is shown in five charts for readability: left lower body, right lower body, left back upper body and sleeve, left front upper body and sleeve, and right front upper body and sleeve.

• Work the large stepped shapes and 9-stitch purple squares of charts in stockinette stitch intarsia (see Glossary, page 135), twisting the yarns at color changes to avoid leaving holes. The short horizontal and vertical lines, small orange circle motifs, and diagonal lines of single stitches are added with duplicate stitch (see Glossary, page 133) after the knitting is complete.

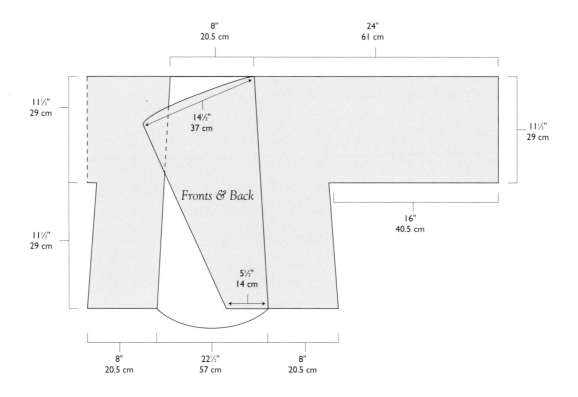

8"
20.5 cm

24"
61 cm

11½"
29 cm

14½"
37 cm

11½"
29 cm

Fronts & Back

16"
40.5 cm

11¼"
29 cm

5½"
14 cm

8"
20.5 cm

22½"
57 cm

8"
20.5 cm

Kimono Left Half

Left Lower Body

With larger cir needle, waste yarn and ribbon, and using the ribbon method provisional cast-on (see Glossary, page 131), CO 80 sts. Joining colors as necessary and beg with RS Row 1, work Rows 1–80 of Left Lower Body chart (see page 36) in St st intarsia (see Notes). With RS facing, place first 40 sts of row on holder or waste yarn for lower left back—40 sts rem for left front; piece measures about 11½" (29 cm) from beg.

Left Front Upper Body and Sleeve

Using the ribbon method provisional cast-on, with RS facing, CO 80 sts at the beg of the sts on the needle so that the first group of sts to be worked on the next RS row will be the 80 new CO sts—120 sts total. Joining colors as necessary and beg with RS Row 81, work Rows 81–160 of Left Front Upper Body and Sleeve chart—piece measures about 23" (58.5 cm) from beg. Mark each end of last row completed with waste yarn to indicate shoulder line.

Left Back Upper Body and Sleeve

Change to Left Back Upper Body and Sleeve chart (see page 37), and work Rows 161–239 *only*. On WS Row 240 of chart, work to end in patt, then place last 80 sts just worked on holder or waste yarn for sleeve "seam"—40 sts rem for upper left back; piece measures about 11½" (29 cm) from marked shoulder line.

Left Lower Body

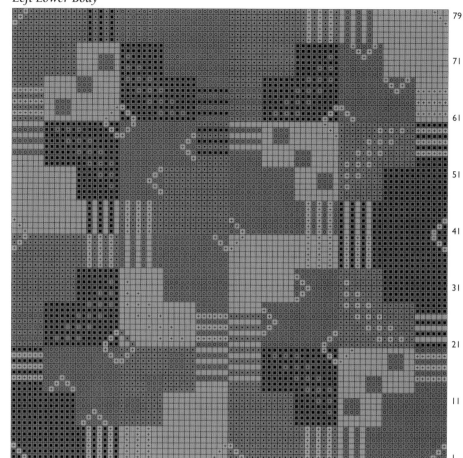

dark olive (MC)

orange-red

purple

brown

orange

Left Front Upper Body and Sleeve

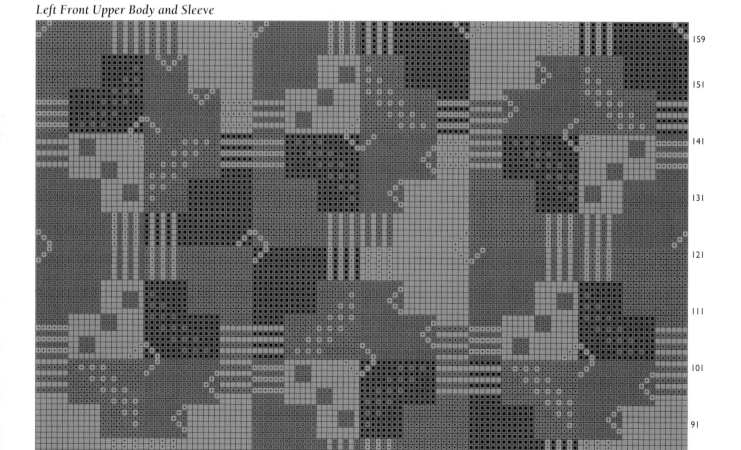

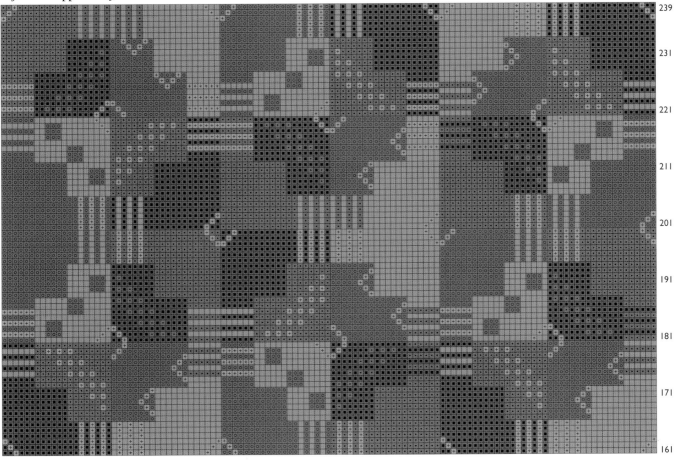

Join Left Upper and Lower Bodies

With yarn threaded on a tapestry needle, and matching background color of one of each pair of blocks to be joined, graft the 40 live sts of the upper left back to the tops of the 40 held sts of lower left back (see Glossary, page 134).

Join Left Sleeve Seam

Carefully remove waste yarn from base of provisional CO for left sleeve, and with matching yarn threaded on a tapestry needle, use the Kitchener st to graft 80 sts at base of CO to tops of 80 held sts for left sleeve. Weave in loose ends.

Kimono Right Half

Right Lower Body

With larger cir needle, waste yarn and ribbon, and using the ribbon method provisional cast-on, CO 80 sts. Joining colors as necessary and beg with RS Row 1, work Rows 1–80 of Right Lower Body chart (see page 38). With RS facing, place last 40 sts of row on holder or waste yarn for lower right back—40 sts rem for right front; piece measures about 11½" (29 cm) from beg.

Right Front Upper Body and Sleeve

Using the ribbon method provisional cast-on and with RS facing, CO 80 sts at the end of the sts on the needle so that the first group of sts to be worked on the next RS row will be the 40 original right front sts—120 sts total. Joining colors as necessary and beg with RS Row 81, work Rows 81–160 of Right Front Upper Body and Sleeve chart—piece measures about 23" (58.5 cm) from beg. Mark each end of last row completed with waste yarn to indicate shoulder line.

Right Back Upper Body and Sleeve

Rep Rows 81–159 of Right Front Upper Body and Sleeve chart once more. On WS Row 160 of chart, work 80 sts in patt, place the 80 sts just worked on a holder or waste yarn for sleeve "seam," work to end in patt—40 sts rem for upper right back; piece measures about 11½" (29 cm) from marked shoulder line.

Join Right Upper and Lower Bodies

With yarn threaded on a tapestry needle, graft the 40 live sts of the upper right back to the tops of the 40 held sts of lower right back.

Right Lower Body

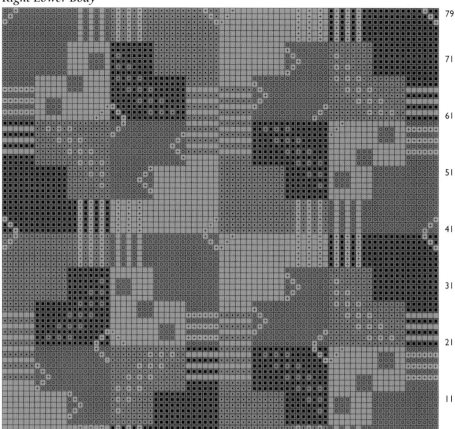

dark olive (MC)

● orange-red

○ purple

■ brown

+ orange

79
71
61
51
41
31
21
11
1

Right Front Upper Body and Sleeve

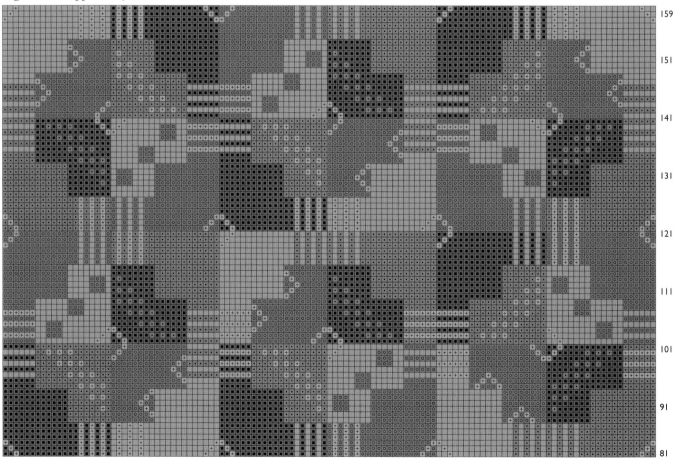

159
151
141
131
121
111
101
91
81

Join Right Sleeve Seam

Carefully remove waste yarn from base of provisional CO for right sleeve, and with matching yarn threaded on a tapestry needle, use the Kitchener st to graft 80 sts at base of CO to tops of 80 held sts for right sleeve. Weave in loose ends.

Prepare Lining

Using one kimono half as a template, cut two identical L-shaped pieces from lining. Turn one lining piece over so the other side of the fabric is facing up, and use the turned-over lining piece as a template to cut two more lining pieces that are mirror images of the first two. With right sides of fabric touching, sew two lining pieces together along the shoulder line, sleeve seam, and side seam with ½" (1.3 cm) seam allowances. Sew the rem two lining pieces tog in the same way, making sure to assemble them so you have both a right and a left lining. Turn lining halves right side out, and finger-press or iron all seams. Set aside.

Embroidery and Beads

Using colors shown on charts threaded on a tapestry needle, embroider short one-row horizontal lines, short one-stitch vertical lines, and small orange circular motifs using duplicate stitch (see Notes) on right and left halves of kimono. For diagonal lines of single stitches, embroider 2 of the 3 diagonal lines, randomly decid-ing which line to omit each time. With sewing needle and thread, sew a line of orange round glass beads on red stepped blocks or brown metal pony beads on brown blocks, to take the place of the omitted line of duplicate sts. Sew a purple cube bead in the center of each 9-stitch purple square. Sew a bronze pony bead or orange glass lentil in the gap of each incomplete small orange circle motif.

Center Back Panel

With MC, RS facing, and shorter, smaller cir needle, pick up and knit 120 sts (about 3 sts for every 4 rows) along center back of left half between lower edge and marked shoulder line. Knit 1 WS row. Cont in short-rows (see Glossary, page 136) as foll:

Rows 1–4: Work in rev St st (purl RS rows, knit WS rows) across all sts, ending with a WS row.

Row 5: (RS) K20, wrap next st, turn.

Even-numbered Rows 6–14: Purl to end.

Odd-numbered Rows 7–13: Knit to wrapped st, work wrapped st tog with its wrap, k19, wrap next st, turn.

Row 15: Knit to wrapped st, work wrapped st tog with its wrap, knit to last 10 sts, wrap next st, turn.

Row 16: Purl to end.

Rep Rows 1–16 ten more times, then work 4 rows even in rev St st—180 rows in short-row sequence at lower edge (beg of RS rows); 48 rows in short-row sequence at neck edge (end of RS rows). Place sts on holder or spare cir needle. With MC, RS facing, and other smaller cir needle, pick up and knit 120 sts (about 3 sts for every 4 rows) along center back of right half between marked shoulder line and lower edge. With RS facing and MC threaded on a tapestry needle, use the Kitchener stitch to graft picked-up sts of right half to live sts of center back panel.

Center Front Panel

With MC, RS facing, and shorter, smaller cir needle, pick up and knit 120 sts (about 3 sts for every 4 rows) along front edge of left half between marked shoulder line and lower edge. Knit 1 WS row. Rep Rows 1–16 of center back panel a total of 7 times, then work 4 rows of rev St st across all sts—116 rows in short-row sequence at neck edge (beg of RS rows); 32 rows in short-row sequence at lower edge (end of RS rows). BO all sts.

Lower Left Facing

Carefully remove waste yarn from 80 sts at base of provisional CO for lower left body and return sts to larger cir needle. Join MC with RS facing. Using shorter, smaller cir needle, knit across 80 sts from base of left lower body. Knit 1 WS row for fold line. Work in St st for 10 rows—facing measures about

1" (2.5 cm) from fold line. BO all sts loosely. Turn facing to WS along fold line and sew invisibly in place with MC.

Back Neck and Right Facing

Carefully remove waste yarn from 80 sts at base of provisional CO for lower right body and return sts to shorter, smaller cir. Join MC with RS facing. Using longer smaller cir, knit across 80 sts from base or lower right body CO, place marker (pm) for lower right front corner, pick up and knit 120 sts along right front edge (about 3 sts for every 4 rows), pm for right neck corner, pick up and knit 40 sts along neck selvedge of upper back panel (about 5 sts for every 6 rows), pm for left neck corner, use the knitted method (see Glossary, page 131) to CO 8 sts—248 sts total. Knit 1 WS row for fold line.

Row 1: (RS) Knit to 2 sts before lower right front corner marker, ssk, slip marker (sl m), k2tog, *knit to 1 st before neck corner m, k1f&b (see Glossary, page 135), sl m, k1f&b; rep from * once more, knit to end—250 sts; 2 sts inc'd at each neck corner, 2 sts dec'd at lower front corner.

Row 2: *Purl to 1 st before corner marker, p1f&b (see Glossary, page 135), sl m, p1f&b; rep from * once more, purl to lower corner marker, p2tog, sl m, ssp (see Glossary, page 133), purl to end—252 sts.

Row 3: Rep Row 1—254 sts.

Row 4: Purl all sts.

Rows 5–8: Rep Rows 1–4 once more—260 sts after completing Row 7.

Rows 9 and 10: Rep Rows 1 and 2 once—264 sts. BO all sts loosely.

With sewing needle and thread, tack grosgrain ribbon along the back neck edge to prevent the neck from stretching out of shape. Turn facing to WS along fold line, enclosing grosgrain ribbon at back neck, and sew invisibly in place with MC threaded on a tapestry needle.

Cuff Facings

With shorter, smaller cir needle, MC, and RS facing, pick up and knit 120 sts (about 3 sts for every 4 rows) along sleeve selvedge at cuff opening. Place marker (pm) and join for working in the rnd. Purl 1 rnd for fold line, then knit 14 rnds for cuff facing. BO all sts loosely. Turn facing to WS along fold line and sew invisibly in place with MC. Rep for other sleeve.

Finishing

Buttonhole

Fold the upper edge of the center front panel down about 2¹⁄₂" (6.5 cm) at its outermost point. Pin through both layers 1¹⁄₂" (3.8 cm) down from the folded edge and 1¹⁄₂" (3.8 cm) in from the BO edge. Where these two pins meet, carefully snip one side

of a single st in the top layer, then turn the piece over and snip 1 side of a single st in the bottom layer. Carefully widen the hole until it is just barely big enough for your chosen button. With MC threaded on a tapestry needle, work buttonhole stitch (see Glossary page 133) around the buttonhole through both layers to secure all the open sts.

Front Crochet Edging

With crochet hook and MC, work a row of reverse single crochet (see Glossary, page 132) along the lower edge of the center front panel and along its BO edge to the upper edge fold, crocheting through both layers of fold in the last 2¹⁄₂" (6.5 cm). *Note:* Folded edge of upper front and lower

edge of center back panel do not have crochet edgings.

Weave in loose ends. Wash in cold water using mild soap or shampoo and rinse with hair conditioner. Lay flat to dry. When slightly damp, steam-block lightly on WS.

Attach Lining

Pin one lining half in place, turning the raw edges under as required to meet the BO edges of the facings and the pick-up rows at center back. Allow lining to blouse slightly at lower edges and cuffs to accommodate stretching of the garment when worn. With sewing needle and thread, slip-stitch (see Glossary, page 136) lining in place around all edges of each intarsia kimono half, leaving

solid-color center front and back panels unlined.

Try on kimono and attach button wherever the best fit is achieved. For the sample shown, the button is 6" (15 cm) down from the right shoulder line.

Cap

Using a beading needle, thread about half of the beads on each ball of yarn before beginning. With larger needles, waste yarn and ribbon, and using the ribbon method provisional cast-on (see Glossary, page 131), CO 40 sts. Change to main yarn and purl 1 WS row without beads. Work beaded patt in short-rows (see Glossary, page 136) as foll:

Row 1: (RS) K1, [place bead in st (see Stitch Guide), k2] 11 times, place bead in st, k1, ending 4 sts from end of row, wrap next st, turn.

Rows 2 and 4: (WS) Purl to end without placing any beads.

Row 3: K2, [place bead in st, k2] 10 times, ending 8 sts from end of row, wrap next st, turn.

Row 5: P1, [place bead between sts (see Stitch Guide), p3] 9 times, ending 12 sts from end of row, wrap next st, turn.

Rows 6 and 8: Knit to end without placing any beads.

Row 7: P2, [place bead between sts, p3] 7 times, place bead between sts, p1, ending 16 sts from end of row, wrap next st, turn.

Row 9: K1, *place bead in st, k2; rep from * to end, working wrapped sts tog with their wraps when you come to them.

Rows 10 and 12: Purl to end without placing any beads.

Row 11: K2, [place bead in st, k2] 11 times, place bead in st, ending 4 sts from end of row, wrap next st, turn.

Row 13: P1, [place bead between sts, p3] 10 times, place bead between sts, p1, ending 8 sts from end of row, wrap next st, turn.

Rows 14 and 16: Knit to end without placing any beads.

Row 15: P2, [place bead between sts, p3] 8 times, place bead between sts, p2, ending 12 sts from end of row, wrap next st, turn.

Row 17: K1, [place bead in st, k2] 7 times, place bead in st, k1, ending 16 sts from end of row, wrap next st, turn.

Rows 18 and 20: Purl to end without placing any beads.

Row 19: K2, *place bead in st, k2; rep from * to last 2 sts, working wrapped sts tog when you come to them, place bead in st, k1.

Row 21: P1, [place bead between sts, p3] 11 times, place bead between sts, p2, ending 4 sts from end of row, wrap next st, turn.

Rows 22 and 24: Knit to end without placing any beads.

Row 23: P2, [place bead between sts, p3] 10 times, ending 8 sts from end of row, wrap next st, turn.

Row 25: K1, [place bead in st, k2] 9 times, ending 12 sts from end of row, wrap next st, turn.

Rows 26 and 28: Purl to end without placing any beads.

Row 27: K2, [place bead in st, k2] 7 times, place bead in st, ending 16 sts from end of row, wrap next st, turn.

Row 29: P1, *place bead between sts, p3; rep from * to end, working wrapped sts tog with their wraps when you come to them.

Rows 30 and 32: Knit to end without placing any beads.

Row 31: P2, [place bead between sts, p3] 11 times, place bead between sts, p1, ending 4 sts from end of row, wrap next st, turn.

Row 33: K1, [place bead in st, k2] 10 times, place bead in st, ending 8 sts from end of row, wrap next st, turn.

Rows 34 and 36: Purl to end without placing any beads.

Row 35: K2, [place bead in st, k2] 8 times, place bead in st, k1, ending 12 sts from end of row, wrap next st, turn.

Row 37: P1, [place bead between sts, p3] 7 times, place bead between sts, p2, ending 16 sts from end of row, wrap next st, turn.

Row 38: Knit to end without placing any beads.

Row 39: P2, *place bead between sts, p3; rep from * to last 2 sts, working wrapped sts tog with their wraps as you come to them, place bead between sts, p2.

Row 40: Knit to end without placing any beads.

Rep Rows 1–40 three more times—160 patt rows total. Leave sts on needle.

Carefully remove waste yarn and ribbon from provisional CO and place live sts on a needle. With main yarn threaded on a tapestry needle, graft live sts to base of provisional CO (see Glossary, page 134). Using yarn tail, close up small opening in center of crown.

Ribbing

With smaller dpn and RS facing, pick up and knit 3 sts for every set of 4 rows of St st or rev St st along selvedge of cap—120 sts total. Place marker (pm), and join for working in the rnd. Work k1, p1 rib for 10 rnds. With yarn threaded on a tapestry needle and using the sewn method (see Glossary, page 130), BO all sts.

Finishing

Weave in all loose ends.

Wash in cold water with a mild soap or shampoo and rinse with a conditioner. Lay flat to dry. When slightly damp, block lightly on WS with a steam iron.

Black and White Handbag

The pattern on this black-and-white hand-bag came from a highly stylized motif on an ancient Huari tunic. The bag is knitted in the round entirely in black with short-rows used to shape the rounded base. After the knitting is complete, the white pattern is added with embroidery. The handle is made up of two knitted cords that are stabilized with nonstretching piping cores and sewn to the sides and bottom of the bag. The embroidered section folds over to one side to close the bag. To prevent small items from pushing through the knitted fabric, the inside of the bag is lined with black silk.

Finished Size 15" (38 cm) wide and about 12" (30.5 cm) tall, with flap folded over.

Yarn CYCA #5 Bulky (chunky weight). *Shown here:* Plymouth Baby Alpaca Grande (100% baby alpaca; 110 yd [101 m]/100 g): #500 black (MC), 3 skeins; #100 off-white (CC), 1 skein.

Needles Bag—size 9 (5.5 mm): straight. I-cord for strap—size 10½ (6.5 mm): 2 double-pointed (dpn). Adjust needle size if necessary to obtain the correct gauge.

Notions Tapestry needle; smooth contrasting waste yarn; 1¾ yd (1.75 m) of 45" (114 cm) quilt batting; 1 yd (1 m) of 45" (114 cm) lining fabric; sharp-point sewing needle and matching thread for lining; 2 yd (m) each of white and black ⅛" (3 mm) piping for core of straps; size H/8 (5.0 mm) crochet hook.

Gauge 12½ sts and 18 rows = 4" (10 cm) in St st using smaller needles.

Notes
• The bag is worked in one piece from the top edge of the front, down to the bottom (where the lower corners are shaped with short-rows), then up to the top edge of the back.

• After the side seams are sewn, the bag will be shaped like a long, thin pouch with embroidery decorating one side of the upper section. Attaching the straps partway up the sides of the pouch will allow the embroidered upper section to fold over the bag front to close the bag.

Bag

Front

With black and smaller needles, CO 46 sts. Work St st until piece measures about 18½" (47 cm) from CO, ending with a WS row.

Shape Lower Corners

Work short-rows (see Glossary, page 136) in St st to shape corners as foll:

Row 1: (RS) K44 to last 2 sts, wrap next st, turn.

Row 2: P42 to last 2 sts, wrap next st, turn.

Row 3: Knit to 2 sts before previous wrapped st, wrap next st, turn.

Row 4: Purl to 2 sts before previous wrapped st, wrap next st, turn.

Rows 5–12: Rep Rows 3 and 4 four more times—12 wrapped sts total; 6 wrapped sts at each side, 22 sts at center between innermost wrapped sts.

Row 13: Knit to end, working wrapped sts tog with their wraps.

Row 14: Purl across all sts, working rem wrapped sts tog with their wraps—piece measures about 21½" (54.5 cm) from CO, measured straight up the center of the piece at tallest point. Mark each end of Row 14 with waste yarn to indicate fold line for bottom of bag.

Row 15: (RS) K34 to last 12 sts, wrap next st, turn.

Row 16: K22 to last 12 sts, wrap next st, turn.

Row 17: Knit to wrapped st, work wrapped st tog with its wrap, k1, wrap next st, turn.

Row 18: Purl to wrapped st, work wrapped st tog with its wrap, p1, wrap next st, turn.

Rows 19–26: Rep Rows 17 and 18 four more times—last wrapped st at each side is the 2nd st in from each end of the row when viewed with RS facing.

Row 27: Knit to end, working wrapped st tog with its wrap.

Row 28: Purl to end, working rem wrapped st tog with its wrap.

Back

Cont in St st until piece measures 43" (109 cm) from CO, measured straight up the center of the piece, and about 18½" (47 cm) from last short-row. BO all sts.

Embroidery

With waste yarn, mark off the embroidery area shown on the Embroidery chart as follows: Beg between the 2 center sts of CO edge of front, stitch a vertical basting line for 40 rows up the center of the piece—23 sts on each side of basting line. Stitch a horizontal basting line above the 40th row of the front to indicate the top of the embroidery area. The embroidery motif is 22 sts wide and 40 rows high; each square on the chart represents 1 knit st of the bag. The solid white areas indicate sts that are to be embroidered in woven stitch embroidery (see Glossary, page 134). Work the motif once

Embroidery

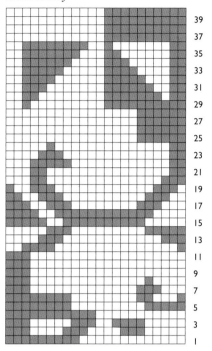

over the 22 sts on each side of the center basting line; do not embroider the selvedge sts—they will be used for seaming. With off-white threaded on a tapestry needle, and following Row 1 of the chart, weave the yarn across the first row of knitting from right to left, working over half a knit st, then under half a knit st, for every white square of the diagram. At the end of each section, reverse direction and work back across the next section, alternating the manner in which you weave over and under half of each st. Carry the yarn loosely across the back of the work to skip over any sts indicated by dark squares. When Row 40 of the first motif has been completed, embroider the motif again on the other side of the center basting line. Secure all ends on WS and remove basting yarn.

Finishing

Fold bag in half along bottom fold line. With black threaded on a tapestry needle, sew side seams, removing waste yarn markers. With black and crochet hook, work reverse single crochet (see Glossary, page 132) around opening at top edge of bag. Weave in all loose ends.

Wash in cold water with mild soap or shampoo and rinse with hair conditioner. Lay flat to dry. When slightly damp, block lightly on WS with a steam iron.

Lining

Trace outline of bag 4 times on lining fabric and cut out all 4 lining pieces. Using the bag as a template, cut 2 pieces of quilt batting in the same manner. With right sides held tog and using a sewing needle and thread, sew 2 pieces of lining tog along the side and bottom edges, leaving the top open. Turn lining right side out and insert one piece of batting. Rep for rem 2 lining pieces and rem piece of batting—2 batting "sandwiches" completed. If desired, sew several lines of quilting sts through all layers to prevent batting from shifting. Place the two lining units one on top of the other, and using sewing needle and thread, sew them tog around sides and bottom. Turn handbag inside out. Match the bottom straight fold line of the bag to the straight edge at the bottom of the joined lining units, and with sewing needle and thread, stitch bag to lining units tog across the bottom. Turn bag right side out to enclose the lining. If necessary, trim the batting so it does not extend beyond the top of the bag. Turn the lining raw edges under ½" (1.3 cm) at the top of each lining unit, and slip-stitch (see Glossary, page 136) top of each lining unit closed. With sewing needle and thread, stitch top edge of lining units to top edge of bag, just below the crochet edging.

I-cord Strap

With black and larger dpn, CO 4 sts. Work 4-st I-cord (see Glossary, page 135) until piece measures 72" (183 cm). Place sts on holder. Rep with white. With matching color of piping threaded on tapestry needle or safety pin, thread piping up the center of each I-cord. Twist the two cords around each other, and use a tapestry needle to graft the live sts at end of each cord to the CO sts of the same cord (see Glossary, page 134). Measure up about 12" (30.5 cm) from fold line at bottom of bag along seam at each side and mark with waste yarn. With yarn threaded on a tapestry needle, sew strap to sides and bottom of bag, beg at one side marker, working down around the bottom of bag, and up to the other side marker, leaving rest of strap free for handle. Fold embroidered top half of bag down to serve as a flap closure.

Embroidered-Back Cardigan and Crocheted Beads

I nspired by a Lambayeque tapestry, the embroidered panel on the back of this flattering blue cardigan offers a surprising flash of colorful detail. The cardigan is worked in a single piece that begins at the left front, continues around the back, and ends at the right front, with short-rows used to shape the body and sleeves along the way. A simple stitch pattern is worked throughout to give the fabric a slightly tweedy texture. The beads are crocheted and strung with assorted glass beads and sequins.

Finished Size Cardigan: 38 (42, 46)" (96.5 [106.5, 117] cm) bust circumference. Large bead necklace: about 36" (91.5 cm) long with 1⅛" (3 cm) diameter beads. Small bead necklace: about 52" (132 cm) long with ¾" (2 cm) diameter beads.

Yarn CYCA #3 Light (DK weight). *Shown here:* The Alpaca Yarn Company Classic Alpaca (100% superfine alpaca; 110 yd [100 m]/50 g): #1627 royal (MC), 16 (17, 19) skeins for cardigan; #1630 parrot (medium blue), #1822 lavender (light purple), #1800 Ozark purple (dark purple), #1819 Victorian rose (medium pink), and #1821 brambleberry (dark pink), 1 skein each for cardigan embroidery. Small amount of each yarn for beads. CYCA #3 Light (DK). *Shown here:* Alpaca with a Twist Baby Twist (100%

baby alpaca; 110 yd [100 m]/50 g): #1006 nautical blue (blue-black) and #1005 cornflower (light blue), 1 skein each for embroidery on cardigan; small amount of each for beads.

Needles Body and sleeves—size 9 (5.5 mm): 32" (60 cm) circular (cir). Facings—size 6 (4 mm): 32" (60 cm) cir and set of 4 or 5 double-pointed (dpn). Adjust needle size if necessary to obtain the correct gauge.

Notions Cardigan: Tapestry needle; markers (m); a few yards (meters) of waste yarn and smooth, satin ribbon for provisional cast-on; stitch holders; four ⅞" (2.2 cm) buttons to decorate lapels; one 10 × 12" (25.5 × 30.5 cm) piece of 11-count Aida cloth; ½ yd (.5 meter) of lining fabric to match MC; sharp-point sewing needle and thread matching MC

for attaching embroidered panel and lining; size 18 tapestry or crewel needle for embroidery. Beads: Size C/2 (2.75 mm) crochet hook; lock-ring marker or safety pin; polyester fiberfill for stuffing beads; tapestry needle; beading needle; beading thread in coordinating color; assorted glass beads and sequins (shown: small iridescent seed beads, ⅜" [1 cm] matte bugle beads, slightly larger iridescent seed beads, ⅛" [3 mm] matte square beads, matte bronze pony beads, and ¼" [6 mm] purple sequins).

Gauge Cardigan: 19½ sts and 42 rows = 4" (10 cm) in nubbly tweed st using larger needle. Beads: about 6 sts and 5 rnds = 1" (2.5 cm) in single crochet (sc). Exact gauge is not critical for beads.

Stitch Guide

Nubbly Tweed: (odd number of sts)

Set-up row: (WS) P1, *k1, p1; rep from * to end.

Row 1: (RS) K1, *sl 1 purlwise with yarn in back (sl 1 pwise wyb), k1; rep from * to end.

Row 2: K1, *p1, k1; rep from * to end.

Row 3: K2, sl 1 pwise wyb, *k1, sl 1; rep from * to last 2 sts, k2.

Row 4: P1, *k1, p1; rep from * to end.

Repeat Rows 1–4 for pattern; do *not* repeat the set-up row.

Notes

• The body of this garment is worked in one piece from side to side, beginning at the left front edge and ending at the right front edge.

• Although the cardigan is worked in one piece, the schematic shows the sleeve separately for clarity. Garment sections are shown oriented in the direction in which they are knitted.

• The finished lengths of the body and sleeves are the same for all sizes. To customize sleeve length, CO more or fewer sts in the first cast-on row for each sleeve; every 5 stitches added or subtracted will lengthen or shorten the sleeve by about 1" (2.5 cm). Keep track of any changes so you can reverse the shaping for the second half of the sleeve and make the other sleeve to match.

Left Front

With larger cir needle, waste yarn and ribbon, and using the ribbon method provisional cast-on (see Glossary, page 131), CO 101 sts. Change to MC and work in nubbly tweed patt until piece measures 4½ (5½, 6½)" (11.5 [14, 16.5] cm) from CO, ending with a WS row.

Shape Left Front Raglan

Work short-rows (see Glossary, page 136) as foll:

Row 1: (RS) Work in patt to last 12 sts, wrap next st, turn.

Even-numbered Rows 2–20: (WS) Work in patt to end.

Odd-numbered Rows 3–21: Work in patt to 2 sts before previous wrapped st, wrap next st, turn.

Row 22: Work in patt to end.

Odd-numbered Rows 23–45: Work in patt to 1 st before previous wrapped st, wrap next st, turn.

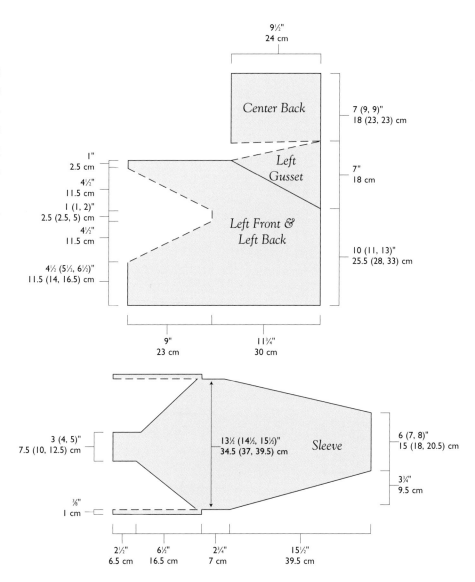

Row 46: Work in patt to end—piece measures about 9 (10, 11)" (23 [25.5, 28] cm) from CO at longer selvedge (beg of RS rows), and about 4½ (5½, 6½)" (11.5 [14, 16.5] cm) from CO at shorter selvedge (end of RS rows); 44 sts total in short-rowed section for raglan.

Next row: (RS) Work in patt across all sts, working wrapped sts tog with their wraps. On the foll WS row, p44, place the 44 sts just worked on holder or waste yarn, work in patt to end—57 sts rem. Work even in patt on 57 sts for 10 (10, 22) more rows—piece measures about 10 (11, 13)" (25.5 [28, 33] cm) from CO at longer

selvedge. Place sts on separate holder.

Left Sleeve

Return 44 held raglan sts of left front to larger needle and rejoin MC with RS facing. Work even in St st for 4 rows, ending with a WS row.

Shape Sleeve and Left Front Raglan

Row 1: Using the cable method (see Glossary, page 131), CO 13 sts, work 13 newly cast-on sts in nubbly tweed patt, place marker (pm) to divide lower sleeve from raglan area, wrap first st of raglan area, turn.

Even-numbered Rows 2–38: Work

in patt to end, slipping marker when you come to it.

Odd-numbered Rows 3–39: CO 4 sts at beg of row, work in patt to wrapped st, work wrapped st tog with its wrap, wrap next st, turn.

Row 40: Work in patt to end—89 sts total CO for lower sleeve; last wrapped st is 20th st from marker in raglan section; sleeve measures about 3¾" (9.5 cm) measured straight up from first CO row at deepest point.

Odd-numbered Rows 41–47: Work in patt to wrapped st, work wrapped st tog with its wrap, wrap next st, turn.

in patt to 2 sts before previous wrapped st, wrap next st, turn.

Even-numbered Rows 10–16: Work in patt to end—after completing Row 16, last wrapped st is 21st st from marker in raglan section.

Odd-numbered Rows 11–15: Work in patt to 1 st before previous wrapped st, wrap next st, turn

Odd-numbered Rows 17–53: BO 4 sts at beg of row, work in patt to 1 st before previous wrapped st, wrap next st, turn.

Even-numbered Rows 18–54: Work in patt to end—57 sts rem after completing Row 53.

Row 55: BO 13 sts at beg of row, discard m between lower sleeve and raglan sections, work in patt to 1 st before previous wrapped st, wrap next st, turn—44 sts rem.

Row 56: Work in patt to end—sleeve measures about 13½ (14½, 15½)" (34.5 [37, 39.5] cm) high from first sleeve CO measured straight up from initial CO row.

Work 4 rows even in St st on rem 44 sts, ending with a WS row. Cut yarn.

Left Back

With RS facing, pm at beg of left sleeve sts, place 57 held left front sts on same needle so first sts to be worked on next RS row will be the front sts—101 sts total. Rejoin MC with RS facing.

Row 1: Work in patt to m, slip marker (sl m), wrap first st of raglan area, turn.

Even-numbered Rows 42–48: Work in patt to end—after completing Row 48, last wrapped st is 24th st from marker in raglan section.

Odd-numbered Rows 49–55: Work in patt to wrapped st, work wrapped st tog with its wrap, work 1 more st, wrap next st, turn.

Even-numbered Rows 50–56: Work in patt to end—after completing Row 56, last wrapped st is 32nd st from marker in raglan section.

Row 57: Work in patt to end, working rem wrapped st tog with its wrap when you come to it—133 sleeve sts total (including raglan sts); sleeve measures about 1½" (3.8 cm) high from last sleeve CO measured along selvedge at beg of RS rows.

Work 31 (41, 51) rows even in patt on all sts, beg and ending with a WS row—piece measures about 4½ (5½, 6½)" (11.5 [14, 16.5] cm) from last sleeve CO row measured along selvedge at beg of RS rows.

Shape Sleeve and Left Back Raglan

Row 1: Work in patt to last 13 sts, wrap next st, turn.

Even-numbered Rows 2–8: Work in patt to end.

Odd-numbered Rows 3–9: Work

Row 2: Work in patt to last st, wrap last st, turn.

Odd-numbered Rows 3–23: Work in patt to wrapped st, work wrapped st tog with its wrap, wrap next st, turn.

Even-numbered Rows 4–24: Work in patt to 1 st *before* previous wrapped st, wrap next st, turn—when Row 24 has been completed, the last wrapped st in the raglan section is the 12th st from marker, and the last wrapped st in the lower body section is the 12th st from the selvedge.

Odd-numbered Rows 25–43: Work in patt to wrapped st, work wrapped st tog with its wrap, work 1 more st, wrap next st, turn.

Even-numbered Rows 26–44: Work in patt to 2 sts before previous wrapped st, wrap next st, turn—when Row 44 has been completed, the last wrapped st in the raglan section is the 32nd st from marker, and the last wrapped st in the lower body section is the 32nd st from the edge.

Row 45: Work in patt to end, working wrapped st tog with its wrap as you come to it.

Even-numbered Rows 46–54: Work in patt to 2 sts before previous wrapped st, wrap next st, turn.

Odd-numbered Rows 47–55: Work in patt to end.

Row 56: Work in patt to 2 sts before previous wrapped st, wrap next st, turn—piece measures about 5½" (14 cm) from beg of left back measured straight up the middle, and about 1" (2.5 cm) high measured along selvedge at end of RS rows; the last wrapped st in the lower body section is the 44th st from the edge.

Next row: (RS) Work in patt to end. *Next row:* BO 55 sts, work in patt to end of row, working wrapped sts tog with their wraps as you come to them—46 sts rem.

Left Gusset

Cont on 46 sts for gusset as foll:

Row 1: (RS) Work in patt to last 9 sts, wrap next st, turn.

Even-numbered Rows 2–70: Work to end.

Odd-numbered Rows 3–69: Work in patt to 1 st before previous wrapped st, wrap next st, turn—after completing Row 69, the last wrapped st is the 4th st from the beg of the Row with RS facing.

Rows 71 and 72: Work in patt to end, working wrapped sts tog with their wraps as you come to them—piece measures about 7" (18 cm) from start of gusset measured along selvedge at beg of RS rows.

Center Back

Cont on 46 sts, work even in patt until piece measures 7 (9, 9)" (18 [23, 23] cm) from end of left gusset, ending with a WS row.

Right Gusset

Row 1: (RS) Work 2 sts in patt, wrap next st, turn.

Even-numbered Rows 2–70: Work to end.

Odd-numbered Rows 3–69: Work in patt to previous wrapped st, work wrapped st tog with its wrap, wrap next st, turn—after completing Row 69, the last wrapped st is the 37th st from the beg of the row with RS facing.

Rows 71 and 72: Work in patt to end, working rem wrapped st tog with its wrap as you come to it—piece measures about 7" (18 cm) from beg of gusset measured along selvedge at beg of RS rows.

Right Back

Row 1: (RS) Work in patt to end of 46 gusset sts.

Row 2: (WS) Use the cable method to CO 55 sts at beg of row, then work in patt across new sts to last 46 sts, wrap next st, turn—101 sts total.

Odd-numbered Rows 3–9: Work in patt to end.

Even-numbered Rows 4–10: Work in patt to wrapped st, work wrapped st tog with its wrap, work 1 more st, wrap next st, turn—after completing Row 10 the last wrapped st is the 38th st from the beg of the row with RS facing.

Row 11: Work in patt to last 12 sts, wrap next st, turn.

Row 12: Work in patt to wrapped

st, work wrapped st tog with its wrap, work 1 more st, wrap next st, turn.

Odd-numbered Rows 13–31: Work in patt to 2 sts before previous wrapped st, wrap next st, turn.

Even-numbered Rows 14–32: Work in patt to wrapped st, work wrapped st tog with its wrap, work 1 more st, wrap next st, turn—after completing Row 32 the last wrapped sts with RS facing are the 16th st from the beg of the row and the 32nd st from the end of the row.

Odd-numbered Rows 33–55: Work in patt to 1 st before previous wrapped st, wrap next st, turn.

Even-numbered Rows 34–56: Work in patt to wrapped st, work wrapped st tog with its wrap, wrap next st, turn—after completing Row 56 the last wrapped sts with RS facing are the 4th st from the beg of the row and the 44th st from the end of the row; piece measures about 5½" (14 cm) from beg of right back measured straight up the middle, and about 1" (2.5 cm) high measured along selvedge at end of RS rows.

Work 2 rows even across all sts, working rem wrapped sts tog with their wraps as you come to them. With RS facing, place 57 sts for lower body on holder or scrap yarn—44 sts rem.

Right Sleeve
Rejoin MC to beg of 44 sts on needle with RS facing. Work as for left sleeve. Cut yarn and place rem 44 sleeve sts on holder.

Right Front
Return 57 held sts of right back to larger cir needle and join MC with RS facing. Work even in patt for 10 (10, 22) more rows, ending with a WS row—piece measures about 1 (1, 2)" (2.5 [2.5, 5] cm) from beg of right front. Return 44 held sts of right sleeve to end of cir needle with RS facing, and pm between the two groups of sts—101 sts total; the first group to be worked on the next RS row will be the lower body sts.

Row 1: (RS) Work 57 sts in patt to m, sl m, wrap first raglan st, turn.

Even-numbered Rows 2–22: Work in patt to end.

Odd-numbered Rows 3–23: Work in patt to previous wrapped st, work wrapped st tog with its wrap, wrap next st, turn.

Row 24: Work in patt to end.

Odd-numbered Rows 25–43: Work in patt to previous wrapped st, work wrapped st tog with its wrap, work 1 more st, wrap next st, turn.

Even-numbered Rows 26–44: Work in patt to end.

Rows 45 and 46: Work in patt to end, working rem wrapped st tog with its wrap on Row 45.

Work even in patt across all sts

until piece measures 4½ (5½, 6½)" (11.5 [14, 16.5] cm) from last short-row, ending with a WS row. Place sts on holder.

Body Facing
With MC, smaller cir needle, and using the cable method, CO 31 (41, 41) sts. Knit across 31 (41, 41) cast-on sts to create a bridge across the gap at top edge of center back, then with RS facing, pick up and knit about 1 st for each st and 1 st for every 2 rows around entire edge of garment body as foll: 5 sts from top edge of left back, 2 sts in 4-row St st left back raglan line, 15 (21, 26) sts across top of left sleeve, 2 sts in left front St st raglan line, 23 (29, 34) sts along top edge of left front, pm. Carefully remove provisional cast-on from 101 sts of left front and return these sts to needle with RS facing. Knit across 101 sts of left front, pm, pick up 53 (58, 68) sts along lower edge of left front to left gusset, 37 sts along lower edge of left gusset, 37 (47, 47) sts along lower edge of center back, 37 sts along lower edge of right gusset, 53 (58, 68) sts along lower edge of right front, pm, return 101 held sts of right front to needle with RS facing, knit across 101 sts of right front, pm, pick up and knit 23 (29, 34) sts along top edge of right front, 2 sts in right front St st raglan line, 15 (21, 26) sts along top edge of right sleeve, 2 sts in right back St st raglan line and

5 sts from top edge of right back—544 (598, 638) sts total. Pm and join for working in the rnd. *Next rnd:* (picot fold line) *K2tog, yo; rep from * to end of rnd. *Dec rnd:* *Knit to 2 sts before corner m, ssk, sl m, k2tog; rep from * 3 more times, knit to end—8 sts dec'd. Work 1 rnd even. Rep the last 2 rnds 5 more times—496 (550, 590) sts; 12 rnds completed after picot fold line.

Upper Corner Facings

The upper corner facings are worked back and forth in short-rows to fill in the corners at the top of each lapel; you may find it helpful to place the surrounding facing sts on waste yarn or holders while working each corner. Slip sts without working them until you are 28 sts before the upper left corner m. Join a new ball of yarn with RS facing. Short-rows for corner will be worked over 56 sts centered on corner (28 sts on each side of corner m) as foll:

Row 1: (RS) Knit to 2 sts before corner m, ssk, sl m, k2tog, k4, wrap next st, turn.

Row 2: (WS) P5 to m, sl m, p5, wrap next st, turn.

Row 3: K3, ssk, sl m, k2tog, k6 working wrapped st tog with its wrap when you come to it, wrap next st, turn.

Row 4: P7 to m, sl m, p7 working wrapped st tog with its wrap when you come to it, wrap next st, turn.

Row 5: K5, ssk, sl m, k2tog, k8 working wrapped st tog with its wrap when you come to it, wrap next st, turn.

Row 6: P9 to m, sl m, p9 working wrapped st tog with its wrap when you come to it, wrap next st, turn.

Row 7: K7, ssk, sl m, k2tog, k10 working wrapped st tog with its wrap when you come to it, wrap next st, turn.

Row 8: P11 to m, sl m, p11 working wrapped st tog with its wrap when you come to it, wrap next st, turn.

Row 9: K9, ssk, sl m, k2tog, k12 working wrapped st tog with its wrap when you come to it, wrap next st, turn.

Row 10: P13 to m, sl m, p13 working wrapped st tog with its wrap when you come to it, wrap next st, turn.

Row 11: K11, ssk, sl m, k2tog, k14 working wrapped st tog with its wrap when you come to it, wrap next st, turn.

Row 12: P15 to m, sl m, p15 working wrapped st tog with its wrap when you come to it, wrap next st, turn.

Row 13: K13, ssk, sl m, k2tog, k16 working wrapped st tog with its wrap when you come to it, wrap next st, turn.

Row 14: P17 to m, sl m, p17 working wrapped st tog with its wrap when you come to it, wrap next st, turn.

Row 15: K15, ssk, sl m, k2tog, k18 working wrapped st tog with its wrap when you come to it, wrap next st, turn.

Row 16: P19 to m, sl m, p19 working wrapped st tog with its wrap when you come to it, wrap next st, turn—16 sts total dec'd at corner, 8 sts dec'd on each side of corner m; last wrapped sts are the 20th sts from corner m. Break yarn.

Slip sts without working them until you are 28 sts before the upper right corner m. Join a new ball of yarn with RS facing, and fill in corner as for upper left corner. When second corner has been filled in, 464 (518, 558) sts rem. Sl sts without working them until you are at beg of the facing rnd again. Knit 1 rnd on all sts, working wrapped sts tog with their wraps. BO all sts.

Collar

With MC and larger cir needle, CO 91 (101, 109) sts. Work even in nubbly tweed patt until piece measures 3¼" (8.5 cm), ending with a WS row. *Next row:* (picot fold line) *K2tog, yo; rep from * to last st, end k1. Beg with a WS row, work even in St st until collar measures 3¼" (8.5 cm) from fold line. BO all sts loosely. Fold collar in half along fold line, and with yarn threaded on a tapestry needle, sew short side seams of collar.

Embroidery

With yarn threaded on an embroidery needle and following the

Embroidery

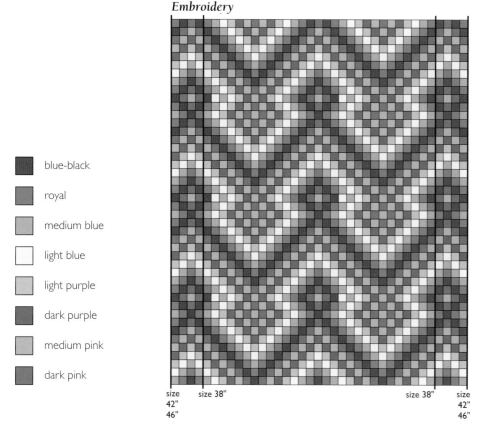

- ■ blue-black
- ■ royal
- ■ medium blue
- □ light blue
- ■ light purple
- ■ dark purple
- ■ medium pink
- ■ dark pink

size 42" 46" | size 38" | size 38" | size 42" 46"

Embroidery chart, work wicker stitch embroidery (see Glossary, page 134) centered on 11-count Aida cloth. Each square of the diagram represents 4 satin stitches, either horizontal or vertical. The finished embroidery area will be 29 (37, 37) blocks wide and 44 blocks high, and will measure about 11" (28 cm) high and 7 (9, 9)" (18 [23, 23] cm) wide. Fold all four edges of Aida cloth to the back along the outer edge of the embroidered area and finger-press in place.

Finishing

Fold body facing to WS along picot fold line, and slip-stitch (see Glossary, page 136) in place with yarn threaded on a tapestry needle.

Cuff Facings

With MC threaded on a tapestry needle, sew sleeve seams, sewing top ½ (½, 1)" (1.3 [1.3, 2.5] cm) of each sleeve selvedge to section worked even for fronts at base of each armhole. With MC, smaller dpn, and RS facing, pick up and knit 34 (38, 44) sts along sleeve selvedge at cuff (about 1 st for every 2 rows of sleeve). Join for working in the rnd and pm to indicate beg of rnd. *Next rnd:* (picot fold line) *K2tog, yo; rep from * to end of rnd. Knit 12 rnds. With size larger cir needle,

BO all sts loosely. Fold facing to WS of sleeve along picot fold line, and slip-stitch in place with yarn threaded on a tapestry needle.

Attach Embroidery

With sewing needle and thread, slip-stitch embroidered panel into rectangular opening at top of center back.

Attach Collar

Center collar along neck edge with nubbly tweed side of collar corresponding to RS of garment and lower edge of collar aligned with body facing slip-stitching. Collar will extend from about the right front raglan to the left front raglan line and the faced edge of the garment will overlap the collar when viewed from the RS. With yarn threaded on a tapestry needle, sew long open side of collar along BO edge of body facing. Fold each upper front corner back as shown to form lapels, and secure by sewing 2 buttons through all layers to each lapel.

Gusset Embroidery

With MC threaded on a tapestry needle, work chain stitch embroidery (see Glossary, page 133) on RS of fabric to outline both gussets. Weave in all loose ends. Wash in cold water with mild soap or shampoo and rinse with hair conditioner. Lay flat to dry. When slightly damp, light steam-block on WS.

Lining

When cardigan is dry, cut a piece of lining fabric 8 (10, 10)" (20.5

[25.5, 25.5] cm) wide and 12" (30.5 cm) high. Turn raw edge of lining under ½" (1.3 cm) to WS around all four sides and finger press in place. With sewing needle and thread, slip-stitch lining to WS of cardigan to cover the wrong side of the embroidered panel.

Large Bead Necklace

Make 3 beads each in each of the 8 colors (24 beads total) as foll:
Ch 4, sl st into first ch st to form a ring. Work 6 sc in ring. Place a lock-ring marker or safety pin after the last sc to indicate end of rnd. Work in rnds as foll, re-positioning the end-of-rnd marker after the final st of each rnd:
Rnd 1: Work 2 sc in each sc around—12 sc.
Rnd 2: Work 2 sc in each sc around—24 sc.
Rnds 3, 4, 5, and 6: Work 1 sc in each sc. Tightly pack polyester fiberfill into center of bead after completing Rnd 6.

Rnd 7: *Work 1 sc in next sc, skip 1 sc; rep from * around—12 sc.
Rnd 8: Rep Rnd 7—6 sc.
Break yarn and fasten off last st. Use yarn tails threaded on tapestry needle to close the openings at top and bottom of bead. Weave ends to inside.

Finishing

With beading thread and needle, string beads as foll, using crochet beads in any color order you choose: *1 sequin, 1 square bead, 1 pony bead, 1 sequin, 1 crochet bead; rep from * until all crochet beads have been used. Tie beading thread securely into a knot, trim the ends to about 2" (5 cm), and run the ends inside the closest crochet bead.

Small Bead Necklace

Work 7 small crochet beads, 1 each in dark navy, medium blue, light blue, dark rose, medium rose, medium purple, and light purple as foll:
Ch 4, sl st into first ch st to form a ring. Work 6 sc in ring. Place a lock-ring marker or safety pin after the last sc to indicate end of rnd. Work in rnds as foll, re-positioning the end-of-rnd marker after the final st of each rnd:
Rnd 1: Work 2 sc in each sc—12 sc. Tightly pack polyester fiberfill into center of bead.

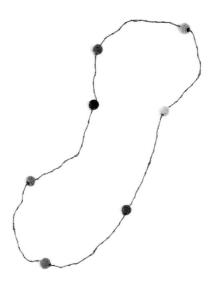

Rnd 2: Work 1 sc in each sc.
Rnd 3: *Work 1 sc in next sc, skip 1 sc; rep from * around—6 sc.
Break yarn and fasten off last st. Use the yarn tails threaded on tapestry needle to close the openings at top and bottom of bead. Weave ends to inside.

Finishing

With beading thread and needle, *string about 7½" (19 cm) of glass beads, 1 sequin, 1 small crochet bead, 1 sequin; rep from * 6 more times, using crochet beads in any color order you choose. For the necklace shown, the beading sequence is: *1 sequin, 1 crochet bead, 1 sequin, 1 larger seed bead, [5 smaller seed beads, 1 bugle bead] 5 times, 5 smaller seed beads, 3 larger seed beads, [5 smaller seed beads, 1 bugle bead] 5 times, 5 smaller seed beads, 1 larger seed bead; rep from * 6 more times. Tie beading thread securely into a knot, trim the ends to about 2" (5 cm), and run the ends inside the closest crochet bead.

People have inhabited the area that is now Peru for thousands of years. Little evidence remains of the earliest settlers, but thanks to the arid coastal climate, artifacts have been uncovered dating back to 1000 B.C. The remnants that have survived indicate that even very early civilizations were accomplished artists.

Paracas

The Paracas culture existed between 600 and 175 B.C. on what is now known as the Paracas Peninsula, about 150 miles south of Lima. This region occupies the northern part of the Nazca Desert, which is arguably the driest desert in the world. Even in the early years of their civilization, the Paracas people were skilled textile producers. Their woven fabrics are characterized by linear patterns following the vertical warp and horizontal weft and by color block patterns of grids of repeating colorful embroidered motifs. To vary the pattern, some of the motifs were rotated or worked in different color combinations. The intricate embroidered motifs commonly represented imaginative flora and fauna and clearly required an astonishing amount of handwork. Because the embroidery was not limited to the vertical and horizontal lines of the warp and weft, the designs exhibit a sense of artistic freedom.

Thousands of Paracas textiles have been recovered from ancient burial sites preserved in the hot, dry desert. The deceased were placed in a sitting position on top

of a number of textiles in a large basket. The basket and the corpse were wrapped in large cotton burial cloths embroidered with llama or alpaca thread. The bundle was topped off with more textiles and offerings of food, jewels, and pottery and covered with additional shrouds. Some bundles—most likely those of the social elite—included more than sixty layers of textiles.

Nazca

The Nazca people, named for the desert region they inhabited along the southern coast of Peru, flourished from about 200 B.C. to about A.D. 600. They supported themselves through farming and fishing and worshiped spiritual powers that controlled the forces of nature. Although the early Nazca period is marked by the introduction of slip-painted pottery, their roots in the Paracas culture meant that embroidery continued to play an important role in their textiles. Motifs included geometric forms as well as abstract natural shapes. Understandably, many Nazca designs reflect a preoccupation with water, which influenced all aspects of desert life. Accomplished Nazca weavers employed a wide color palette, complicated loom techniques involving discontinuous warps and wefts, and exacting embroidery.

Huari

Between about A.D. 700 and 1000, the Huari dominated most of the Andean region, particularly the highlands. In addition to fine ceramics, the Huari produced lively and complicated textiles that involved geometric studies of repetition, abstraction, and fragmentation of individual motifs. Some textiles incorporated extremely delicate threads that crossed each other as many as three hundred times per inch of cloth. The majority of the surviving Huari tapestry tunics feature plain and patterned bands that commonly include stepped motifs (blocks of color offset from each other horizontally and vertically to give the impression of stair steps).

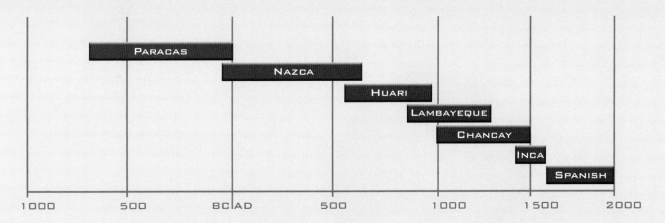

PARACAS
NAZCA
HUARI
LAMBAYEQUE
CHANCAY
INCA
SPANISH

1000   500   BC|AD   500   1000   1500   2000

Lambayeque

The Lambayeque lived along the northern coast of Peru at about the same time the Chancay inhabited the central coast, from about 800 until their defeat by the Incas in the 1400s. This period marks an explosion in art and crafts made with clay, wood, gold, silver, and precious and semiprecious stones. Many of their tapestries are decorated with anthropomorphic figures wearing large headdresses, birds, and geometric motifs.

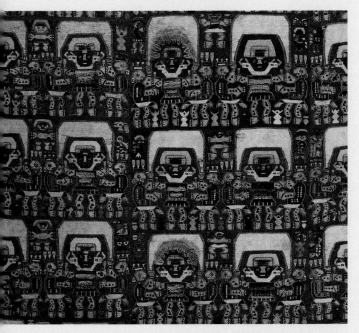

Chancay

The fertile coastal region along central Peru was the home of the advanced Chancay civilization from the 900s until its defeat by the Incas in the 1400s. Although the Chancay produced ceramics, they are best known for their textiles, which include painted cloths, tapestries, brocades, and embroideries. The most notable textiles are the elaborate woven gauzes and lacework.

Their culture was known for a general acceptance of personal expression and individual style, leading to prolific artistic output.

Inca

The Incan empire was the last and best documented empire of pre-Columbian Peru. They dominated the entire region for about a hundred years until they were defeated by the Spanish in the 1500s. This period marked the development of government control over roads, textiles, and agriculture. The state owned vast herds of alpacas and llamas, while citizens were not allowed more than ten of each without royal permission. Restrictions were placed on hunting wild animals, and all vicuña fiber was reserved for royal use. A textile tax made weaving for the state obligatory, and rulers distributed fine textiles in recognition of social status and power. The weavings reveal great technical skill and include fabrics woven with several hundred threads per inch of cloth and impressive weft-faced and double-faced designs. Geometric themes predominated, with eight-pointed stars, diamonds, checkerboards, crosses, and stepped motifs. Tunic styles became standardized, and many included zigzag patterns along the lower edges.

Spanish

Discovery of North America by Christopher Columbus in 1492 marked the end of the pre-Columbian era. In the decades that followed, the Spanish had advanced into South America, and by the early 1500s they conquered the ruling Incas. With the Spaniards came an onslaught of European influences in art, dress, and politics, but this did not completely eradicate the rich cultural identity developed through the ages.

Crocheted Poncho

This airy crocheted poncho takes inspiration from a delicate pre-Incan gauze tapestry that was woven by the Chancay people as long as a thousand years ago. In my version, I used a number of crochet stitches to produce a web of intersecting horizontal and vertical bars to form windowpanes. Tiny ribbon bows and beaded flowers accent the intersections, much like the original tapestry. The poncho is worked in one piece from the lower front edge to the shoulders, then from the shoulders down to the lower back edge, with a slit opening for the neck in the center of the shoulder line. Worked in a delicate Suri alpaca, this drapey piece can be worn as a simple poncho or as a loose blouse if extra lengths of ribbon are threaded and gathered along the shoulders and sides.

Finished Size 40" (101.5 cm) wide and 20" (51 cm) long from shoulder to lower edge.

Yarn CYCA #1 Super Fine (lace weight). *Shown here:* The Alpaca Yarn Company Suri Elegance (100% Suri alpaca; 875 yd [800 m]/100 g): #2205 copper (MC), 1 hank.

Trendsetter Segue (100% polyamide ribbon; 120 yd [110 m]/100 g): #501 azure/green/gold/rust multicolor, 1 skein.

Hook Size E/4 (3.5 mm).

Notions Tapestry needle; beading needle; about 400 ¼" (6-mm) metallic gold bugle beads; 100 iridescent rocaille beads.

Gauge 40 sts and 12 rows (4 reps of main patt) = 4" (10 cm). Exact gauge is not critical for this project.

Notes
• See Glossary, pages 132–133, for crochet instructions (ch, sc, dc, qc).
• The poncho is worked in one piece from the lower front edge to the shoulders, then from the shoulders down to the lower back edge. A slit opening for the neck is worked in the center of the shoulder line.
• Each windowpane opening of the pattern is surrounded by vertical and horizontal "sashing" on all sides. An "intersection" is where the vertical and horizontal sashing meet and can also be identified as the more solid area in the center of a group of 4 windowpanes—2 panes wide by 2 panes high.

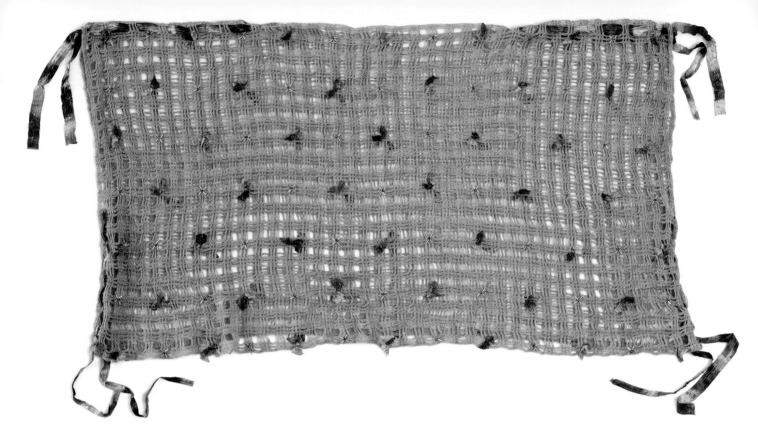

Poncho

Front

With MC, Ch 406 (counts as 404 foundation ch, plus ch-2 turning ch). Work three-tier window st patt as foll:

Row 1: (RS) Sc in 3rd ch from hook, then 1 sc in each ch to end—404 sc.

Row 2: (WS) Ch 3, dc in second sc from end of previous row, ch 1, skip 1 sc, dc in next sc, *ch 5, skip 5 sc, [dc in next sc, ch 1, skip 1 sc] 2 times, dc in next sc; rep from * 39 more times—40 ch-5 spaces.

Row 3: Ch 3, dc in second dc from end of previous row, ch 1, dc in next dc, *ch 5, [dc in next dc, ch 1] 2 times, dc in next dc; rep from * 39 more times, ending with final dc of last rep in 2nd ch of ch-3 at beg of previous row.

Row 4: (windowpane row) Ch 7, qc in second dc from end of previous row, ch 1, qc in next dc, *ch 5, [qc in next dc, ch 1] 2 times, qc in next dc; rep from * 39 more times, ending with final qc of last rep in 2nd ch of ch-3 at beg of previous row.

Row 5: Ch 3, dc in second qc from end of previous row, ch 1, dc in next qc, *ch 5, [dc in next qc, ch 1] 2 times, dc in next qc; rep from * 39 more times, ending with final dc of last rep in 2nd-to-last ch of ch-7 at beg of previous row.

Rows 6–8: Rep Rows 3–5.

Rep Rows 3–8 eight more times, then work Rows 3–6 once more—piece measures about 19½" (49.5 cm) from beg; 60 patt rows completed; 19 vertical windowpane spaces total.

Neck Opening

(Row 7 of patt) Ch 7, qc in second dc from end of previous row, ch 1, qc in next dc, *ch 5, [qc in next dc, ch 1] 2 times, qc in next dc*, rep from * to * 12 more times, ch 135, skip the next 14 ch-5 loops and the 13 [dc, ch 1, dc, ch 1, dc] groups between them, [qc in next dc, ch 1] 2 times, qc in next dc, rep from * to * 13 more times, ending with final qc of last rep in 2nd ch of ch-3 at beg of previous row—13 horizontal windowpane spaces on each side of neck opening.

Back

Work Row 8 of patt, then rep Rows 3–8 nine more times, then work Rows 3–6 once more—59 rows completed after neck opening row; 19 vertical windowpane spaces above neck opening row; 39 vertical windowpane spaces total from beg. *Next row:* Ch 1, work 1 sc in each dc and ch across. Fasten off.

Finishing

Weave in all loose ends.

Wash in cold water with mild soap or shampoo and rinse with hair conditioner. Lay flat to dry. When slightly damp, lightly steam-block on WS.

Beaded Clusters

The poncho has 40 windowpanes

and 41 intersections horizontally including the edges at both sides, and 39 windowpanes and 40 intersections vertically including the top and bottom edges; the beaded clusters and ribbon knots are placed in specific intersections. Placing clusters as described below, work each cluster as foll: Cut a 12" (30.5 cm) length of yarn. Double the strand and thread the ends through the eye of the beading needle. Secure the thread in the center of the desired intersection by taking a small stitch, pass the needle through the loop at the end of the thread, and tighten. Sew 1 rocaille bead over the center anchor point, then sew 4 bugle beads radiating out from the center bead, star-fashion. Fasten off thread securely to WS.

Lay poncho with RS facing and foundation ch of front at lower edge. Clusters are located as foll:

Line 1: In the very first horizontal sash at lower edge (initial Rows 1, 2, and 3 of patt), counting the intersection at the right-hand edge as the first intersection, and counting from right to left, place a cluster in the 6th, 12th, 18th, 24th, 30th, and 36th intersections across.

Line 2: In the fourth horizontal sash from the bottom, and counting from right to left as for Line 1, place a cluster in the 3rd, 9th, 15th, 21st, 27th, 33rd, and 39th intersections across.

Lines 3, 5, and 7: Place clusters as for Line 1 in the 7th, 13th and 19th horizontal sashes from the bottom, respectively.

Lines 4 and 6: Place clusters as for Line 2 in the 10th and 16th horizontal sashes from the bottom, respectively.

Turn poncho upside down with RS still facing and final row of sc at lower edge. Place beaded clusters on back the same as the front.

Ribbon Knots

Cut 92 pieces of ribbon yarn, each 3" (7.5 cm) long. Placing knots as described below, work each knot as foll: With crochet hook, pull one end of ribbon through center of intersection. Even the ends, and tie securely with an overhand knot. Lay poncho with RS facing and foundation ch of front at lower edge. Knots are located as foll:

Line 1: In the very first horizontal sash at lower edge, and counting from right to left, place a knot in the 3rd, 9th, 15th, 21st, 27th, 33rd, and 39th intersections across, exactly centered between each pair of Line 1 beaded clusters where possible.

Line 2: In the fourth horizontal sash from the bottom, and counting from right to left as for Line 1, place a cluster in the 6th, 12th, 18th, 24th, 30th, and 36th intersections across, exactly centered between each pair of Line 2 beaded clusters where possible.

Lines 3, 5, and 7: Place clusters as for Line 1 in the 7th, 13th and 19th horizontal sashes from the bottom, respectively.

Lines 4 and 6: Place clusters as for Line 2 in the 10th and 16th horizontal sashes from the bottom, respectively.

Turn poncho upside down with RS still facing and final row of sc at lower edge. Place knots on back the same as the front.

Shoulder Lacing

(optional) Cut 2 lengths of ribbon yarn, each about 40" (101.5 cm) long. With ribbon threaded on a tapestry needle, and beginning at side edge, weave ribbon through the line of windowpanes along the shoulder line to neck opening. At neck opening, reverse direction and weave through an adjacent line of windowpanes back to the edge. Even the ends of the ribbon, pull gently to gather the shoulder as desired, and tie into a bow. Rep for the other shoulder.

Side Lacing

(optional) Cut 2 lengths of ribbon yarn as for shoulder lacing. Hold the front and back sides tog with WS facing each other so that the first window frames at each side overlap. With ribbon threaded on a tapestry needle, and beginning at lower edge and working upward, weave ribbon through the double layer of windowpanes for about 9 panes, reverse direction, and weave through the same line of windowpanes back to the edge, weaving so that you go over the intersections you previously went under, and vice versa. Even the ends of the ribbon, pull gently to gather the sides as desired, and tie into a bow. Rep for the other side.

Short Cardigan with Ribbon Trim

The knitted lace pattern in this flattering cardigan was based on a delicate Chancay tapestry and was developed especially for this book by Sharon Winsauer. The cropped body is worked in one piece from side to side, beginning at the right front edge and ending at the left front edge, and shaped with short-rows along the way. The lightly textured sleeves are worked downward from the shoulders in a broken rib pattern. A generous ruffle of sheer satin-edge ribbon trims the neck, front, and lower body edges.

Finished Size 36 (41, 44½)" (91.5 [104, 113] cm) bust circumference. *Note:* Front edges of cardigan deliberately do not meet at center front; therefore the garment can accommodate a slightly smaller or larger bust.

Yarn CYCA #4 Medium (worsted weight). *Shown here:* The Fibre Company Fauna White Diamond (50% alpaca, 30% merino, 10% ingeo corn fiber, 10% firestar nylon; 100 yd [91 m]/50 g): off-white, 11 (13, 15) skeins.

Needles Body and sleeves—size 6 (4 mm): 32" (80 cm) circular (cir). Lace ruffle—size 9 (5.5 mm): 32" (80 cm) cir. Adjust needle size if necessary to obtain the correct gauge.

Notions Removable markers (m); tapestry needle; 6 (7, 8) yd (5.5 [6.4, 7.3] m) of 3" (7.5 mm) off-white satin edge organza ribbon (available at fabric and wedding supply stores); sewing needle and thread for attaching ribbon trim; sewing pins; sewing machine (optional) for gathering ribbon.

Gauge 20 sts and 29 rows = 4" (10 cm) in St st using smaller needle; 25 sts and 30 rows = 4" (10 cm) in broken rib patt using smaller needle.

Stitch Guide
Broken Rib Stitch:
(even number of sts)
Row 1: (RS) Knit.
Row 2: (WS) *K1, p1; rep from *.
Repeat Rows 1 and 2 for pattern.
Cross-2: K2tog, leave sts on needle, knit both sts tog again through their back loops, slip both sts from needle. *Note:* Work very loosely to make it easier to work the cross-2 sts on the following row and to maintain the open, lacy quality of the fabric. The single chart symbol for cross-2 represents 2 sts.

K1, sl 1, k1: K1, sl the double yarn-over of the previous row as if to knit with yarn in back, k1. As you slip each double yarnover, drop its extra wrap so only one yarnover loop remains on the needle, leaving an extra-large hole. The single chart symbol for knit 1, slip 1, knit 1 represents 3 sts.

Make hole: Sl the st before the yarn-over as if to knit, insert the right needle tip from front to back under-neath the slip st strand from the previ-ous row and into the yarnover on the needle, k1 allowing the yarnover to drop from the needle, pass slipped st over. Insert the right needle tip from front to back into the yarnover hole again to lift the yarnover and slipped st strands onto the right needle, then insert right needle tip into the next st on left needle, k1 from left needle without drawing the new st through the lifted strands, then pass 2 lifted strands on the right needle over the new knit st. The resulting 2 sts are worked as a cross-2 on the following row. The single chart symbol for this represents 3 sts (the slipped yo and 1 st on either side of it) decreased to 2 sts, with a large hole centered below the 2 rem sts.

Notes

- The main body is worked in one piece from side to side, beginning at the right front edge and ending at the left front edge.
- The size of the lace pattern repeat ranges from 18 to 27 stitches; the stitch count does not remain con-stant from round to round.
- The gray "no stitch" squares on the chart are placeholders that allow the pattern to line up visually. There is no action associated with them; simply skip the gray squares as you come to them.
- Some chart symbols represent 2 or 3 stitches; refer to the Stitch Guide for how to work these stitches.
- If you choose to set off each lace pattern repeat with markers, be aware that you will have to reposi-tion the markers frequently because adjacent repeats loan and borrow stitches to and from each other, and because markers will fall in the center of some cross-2 stitches.

Right Front

With smaller needle, CO 50 (58, 66) sts. Work 2 rows in St st, end-ing with a WS row. Shape right front using short-rows (see Glos-sary, page 136) as foll:

Rows 1 and 3: (RS) Knit to end.

Row 2: (WS) Purl to last 6 sts, wrap next st, turn.

Row 4: Purl to 4 sts before previ-ous wrapped st, wrap next st, turn.

Rep Rows 3 and 4 nine (eleven, thirteen) more times—24 (28, 32) rows completed from CO along selvedge at end of RS rows; final wrapped st is 5th st from end of RS row and 46th (54th, 62nd) st from beg of RS row. Knit to end of next RS row, then purl to end of foll WS row, working all wrapped sts tog with their wraps as you come to them—26 (30, 34) rows completed; piece mea-sures about 3½ (4, 4½)" (9 [10, 11.5] cm) from CO along selvedge at end of RS rows (lower right front edge).

Right Raglan

Mark each end of row with remov-able marker or waste yarn to indicate beg of right raglan. Cont in St st, shape right front raglan using short-rows as foll:

Rows 1 and 3: (RS) Knit to end.

Row 2: P1 (3, 3), wrap next st, turn.

Row 4: Purl to previous wrapped st, work wrapped st tog with its wrap, p1 (3, 3), wrap next st, turn.

Rows 5 and 6: Rep Rows 3 and 4 once.

Row 7: Knit to end.

Row 8: Purl to previous wrapped st, work wrapped st tog with its wrap, p1 (1, 3), wrap next st, turn.

Row 9: Knit to end.

Row 10: Purl to previous wrapped st, work wrapped st tog with its wrap, p1, wrap next st, turn.

Rep Rows 9 and 10 eighteen (nine-teen, twenty-two) more times—46 (48, 54) rows completed from raglan marker along selvedge at end of RS rows; final wrapped st is 5th st from beg of RS row. Knit 1 RS row to end. Working rem wrapped st tog with its wrap when you come to it, work 3 more rows even in St st across all

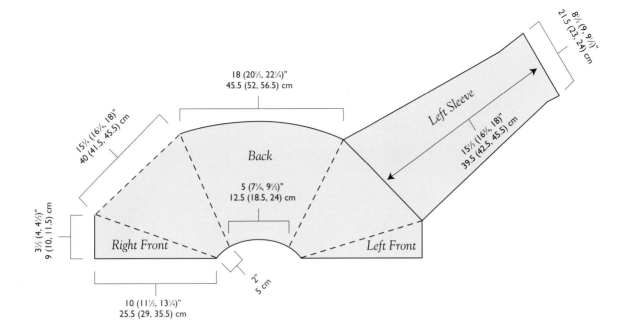

Back

18 (20½, 22¼)"
45.5 (52, 56.5) cm

5 (7¼, 9½)"
12.5 (18.5, 24) cm

15¾ (16¼, 18)"
40 (41.5, 45.5) cm

Left Sleeve

8½ (9, 9½)"
21.5 (23, 24) cm

15½ (16¼, 18)"
39.5 (42.5, 45.5) cm

Right Front

Left Front

3½ (4, 4½)"
9 (10, 11.5) cm

2"
5 cm

10 (11½, 13¼)"
25.5 (29, 35.5) cm

sts, ending with a WS row—50 (52, 58) rows completed from raglan marker along selvedge at end of RS rows. Shape "dart" at top of shoulder using short-rows as foll:

Odd-numbered Rows 1–7: (RS) Knit to end.

Row 2: Purl to last 6 sts, wrap next st, turn.

Row 4: Purl to 6 sts before previous wrapped st, wrap next st, turn.

Row 6: Purl to 8 sts before previous wrapped st, wrap next st, turn.

Row 8: Purl to end, working wrapped sts tog with their wraps as you come to them.

Row 9: Knit to end.

Row 10: Purl to last 20 sts, wrap next st, turn.

Odd-numbered Rows 11–15: Knit to end.

Row 12: Purl to previous wrapped st, work wrapped st tog with its wrap, p7, wrap next st, turn.

Row 14: Purl to previous wrapped st, work wrapped st tog with its wrap, p5, wrap next st, turn.

Row 16: Purl to end, working rem wrapped st tog with its wrap when you come to it.

Work 2 rows even in St st across all sts, ending with a WS row—68 (70, 76) rows completed from raglan marker along selvedge at end of RS rows. Reverse shaping for right back raglan as foll:

Row 1: (RS) Knit to end.

Row 2: Purl to last 5 sts, wrap next st, turn.

Row 3: Knit to end.

Row 4: Purl to 2 sts before previous wrapped st, wrap next st, turn.

Rep Rows 3 and 4 twenty-one (nineteen, twenty-two) more times—114 (112, 124) rows completed from raglan marker along selvedge at end of RS rows; final wrapped st is 49th (45th, 51st) st from beg of RS row. Raglan shaping is completed for size 36". Skip to Back on page 68.

Sizes 41 (44½)" Only

Finish raglan shaping as foll:

Rows 1 and 3: Knit to end.

Row 2: Purl to (2, 4) sts before previous wrapped st, wrap next st, turn.

Row 4: Purl to 4 sts before previous wrapped st, wrap next st, turn.

Rows 5 and 6: Rep Rows 3 and 4 once more—(118, 130) rows completed from raglan marker along selvedge at end of RS rows; with RS facing, final wrapped st is (55th, 63rd) st from beg of row.

Raglan shaping is completed for all sizes. Mark each end of row with removable marker or waste yarn to indicate end of right raglan—piece measures 15¾ (16¼, 18)" (40 [41.5, 45.5] cm) between markers along selvedge at end of RS rows (right sleeve pick-up edge), and about 2" (5 cm) between markers along selvedge at beg of RS rows (neck edge).

Back

Cont in St st, shape right back raglan and curved edges for lower back and back neck as foll:

Rows 1 and 3: (RS) Knit to end.

Row 2: P1 (3, 3), wrap next st, turn.

Row 4: Purl to previous wrapped st, work wrapped st tog with its wrap, p1 (3, 3), wrap next st, turn.

Row 5: Knit to last 3 sts, k1f&b (see Glossary, page 135), k2, turn—1 st inc'd at lower back edge (end of RS rows); 51 (59, 67) sts.

Rows 6 and 7: Rep Rows 4 and 5 once more—52 (60, 68) sts.

Row 8: Purl to previous wrapped st, work wrapped st tog with its wrap, p1 (1, 3), wrap next st, turn.

Row 9: Knit to last 3 sts, k1f&b, k2, turn—1 st inc'd at lower back edge.

Row 10: Purl to previous wrapped st, work wrapped st tog with its wrap, p1, wrap next st, turn.

Rows 11–32: Rep Rows 9 and 10 eleven more times—64 (72, 80) sts after completing Row 31; final wrapped st is 19th (21st, 27th) st from beg of RS row.

Row 33: Knit to end.

Row 34: Purl to previous wrapped st, work wrapped st tog with its wrap, p1, wrap next st, turn.

Row 35: Knit to last 3 sts, k1f&b, k2, turn—1 st inc'd at lower back edge.

Row 36: Purl to previous wrapped st, work wrapped st tog with its wrap, p1, wrap next st, turn.

Rows 37–40: Rep Rows 33–36 once more—66 (74, 82) sts after completing Row 39; final wrapped st is 11th (13th, 19th) st from beg of RS row.

Rows 41 and 43: Knit to end.

Rows 42 and 44: Purl to previous

wrapped st, work wrapped st tog with its wrap, p1, wrap next st, turn.

Row 45: Knit to last 3 sts, k1f&b, k2, turn—1 st inc'd at lower back edge.

Row 46: Purl to previous wrapped st, work wrapped st tog with its wrap, p1, wrap next st, turn—67 (75, 83) sts after completing Row 45; final wrapped st is 5th (7th, 13th) st from beg of RS row.

Cont as foll for your size.

Size 36" Only

Rows 47 and 49: Knit to end.

Rows 48 and 50: Purl to end, working rem wrapped st tog with its wrap when you come to it in Row 48.

Row 51: K2, ssk, knit to last 3 sts, k1f&b, k2—still 67 sts; 1 st dec'd at neck edge (beg of RS rows); 1 st inc'd at lower edge.

Rows 52–54: Work even in St st across all sts.

Row 55: K2, ssk, knit to end—66 sts rem.

Rows 56–58: Work even in St st across all sts.

Row 59: Rep Row 55—65 sts rem.

Rows 60–65: Work even in St st across all sts—this is the center of the back; piece measures about 9" (23 cm) from beg of back at highest point measured along a single column of sts; do not measure along the curve of lower back selvedge.

Rows 66–68: Work even in St st across all sts.

Row 69: K2, k1f&b, knit to end—66 sts.

Rows 70–72: Work even in St st across all sts.

Row 73: Rep Row 69—67 sts.

Rows 74–76: Work even in St st across all sts.

Row 77: K2, k1f&b, knit to last 4 sts, k2tog, k2—still 67 sts; neck shaping completed.

Rows 78–81: Work even in St st across all sts.

Row 82: Purl to last 4 sts, wrap next st, turn. Skip to *All sizes* on page 70.

Size 41" Only

Rows 47 and 49: Knit to end.

Row 48: Purl to previous wrapped st, work wrapped st tog with its wrap, p1, wrap next st, turn—with RS facing, final wrapped st is 5th from beg of row.

Row 50: Purl to end, working rem wrapped st tog with its wrap when you come to it.

Row 51: K2, ssk, knit to last 3 sts, k1f&b, k2—still 75 sts; 1 st dec'd at neck edge (beg of RS rows); 1 st inc'd at lower edge.

Rows 52–54: Work even in St st across all sts.

Row 55: K2, ssk, knit to end—74 sts rem.

Rows 56–58: Work even in St st across all sts.

Row 59: Rep Row 55—73 sts rem.

Rows 60–74: Work even in St st

across all sts—this is the center of the back; piece measures about 10¼" (26 cm) from beg of back at highest point measured along a single column of sts; do not measure along the curved lower back edge.

Rows 75–84: Work even in St st across all sts.

Row 85: K2, k1f&b, knit to end—74 sts.

Rows 86–88: Work even in St st across all sts.

Row 89: Rep Row 85—75 sts.

Rows 90–92: Work even in St st across all sts.

Row 93: K2, k1f&b, knit to last 4 sts, k2tog, k2—still 75 sts; neck shaping completed.

Rows 94–97: Work even in St st across all sts.

Row 98: Purl to last 4 sts, wrap next st, turn. Skip to *All Sizes* on page 70.

Size 44½" Only

Rows 47 and 49: Knit to end.

Rows 48 and 50: Purl to previous wrapped st, work wrapped st tog with its wrap, p1, wrap next st, turn.

Row 51: K2, ssk, knit to last 3 sts, k1f&b, k2—still 83 sts; 1 st dec'd at neck edge (beg of RS rows); 1 st inc'd at lower edge.

Rows 52 and 54: Purl to previous wrapped st, work wrapped st tog with its wrap, p1, wrap next st, turn—final wrapped st is 4th from beg of RS row when Row 54 has been completed.

Row 53: Knit to end.

Row 55: K2, ssk, knit to end—82 sts rem.

Rows 56–58: Work even in St st across all sts.

Row 59: Rep Row 55—81 sts rem.

Rows 60–80: Work even in St st across all sts—this is the center of the back; piece measures about 11" (28 cm) from beg of back at highest point measured along a single column of sts; do not measure along the curved lower back edge.

Rows 81–92: Work even in St st across all sts.

Row 93: K2, k1f&b, knit to end—82 sts.

Rows 94–96: Work even in St st across all sts.

Row 97: Rep Row 93—83 sts.

Rows 98–100: Work even in St st across all sts.

Row 101: K2, k1f&b, knit to last 4 sts, k2tog, k2—still 83 sts; neck shaping completed.

Rows 102–105: Work even in St st across all sts.

Row 106: Purl to last 4 sts, wrap next st, turn.

All Sizes

Reverse shaping for left back raglan and complete lower edge shaping as foll:

Row 1: (RS) Knit to end.

Even-numbered Rows 2–16: Purl to 2 sts before previous wrapped st, wrap next st, turn.

Row 3: Knit to last 4 sts, k2tog, k2—66 (74, 82) sts.

Rows 5 and 7: Knit to end.

Row 9: Rep Row 3—65 (73, 81) sts.

Row 11: Knit to end.

Row 13: Rep Row 3—64 (72, 80) sts.

Row 15: Knit to end.

Row 17: Rep Row 3—63 (71, 79) sts.

Row 18: Purl to 2 sts before previous wrapped st, wrap next st, turn.

Rep Rows 17 and 18 twelve more times—51 (59, 67) sts rem; 124 (140, 148) rows total from beg of back along selvedge at end of RS rows; last wrapped st is 6th (14th, 22nd) st from end of RS row. Complete left back raglan as foll for your size.

Size 36" Only

On the next RS row, knit to last 4 sts, k2tog, k2—50 sts rem. On the foll WS row, purl to 2 sts before previous wrapped st, wrap next st, turn. On next RS row, knit to end. On the foll WS row, purl to 1 st before previous wrapped st, wrap next st, turn—final wrapped st is 2nd st from end of RS row. Work 2 rows even in St st across all sts, working wrapped sts tog with their wraps as you come to them—130 rows total from beg of back along selvedge at end of RS rows; back measures about 18" (45.5 cm) from beg of back at highest point measured along a single column of sts; do not measure along the curve of lower back selvedge. Skip to *Left Raglan.*

Size 41" Only

On next RS row, knit to last 4 sts, k2tog, k2—58 sts rem. On the foll WS row, purl to 2 sts before previous wrapped st, wrap next st, turn. On the next RS row, knit to end. On the foll WS row, purl to 4 sts before previous wrapped st, wrap next st, turn. Rep the last 2 rows once more—final wrapped st is 3rd st from end of RS row. Work 2 rows even in St st across all sts—148 rows total from beg of back along selvedge at end of RS rows; back measures about 20½" (52 cm) from beg of back at highest point measured along a single column of sts; do not measure along the curve of lower back selvedge. Skip to *Left Raglan.*

Size 44½" Only

On next RS row, knit to last 4 sts, k2tog, k2—66 sts rem. On the foll WS row, purl to 2 sts before previous wrapped st, wrap next st, turn. On the next RS row, knit to end. Rep the last 2 rows 2 more times, ending with a RS row. On the foll WS row, purl to 4 sts before previous wrapped st, wrap next st, turn. On the next RS row, knit to end. Rep the last 2 rows 2 more times—final wrapped st is 3rd st from end of RS row. Work 2 rows even in St st, working all wrapped sts tog with their wraps as you come to them, and ending with a WS row—162 rows total from beg of back along selvedge at end of RS rows; back measures about 22¼" (56.5 cm) from beg of back at highest point measured along a single column of sts; do not measure along the curve of lower back selvedge.

Left Raglan

Work as for right raglan.

Left Front

Rows 1 and 3: (RS) Knit to end.

Row 2: P3, wrap next st, turn.

Row 4: Purl to wrapped st, work wrapped st tog with its wrap, p3, wrap next st, turn.

Rep Rows 3 and 4 nine (eleven, thirteen) more times—22 (26, 30) rows completed from beg of left front along selvedge at end of RS rows; final wrapped st is 7th st from beg of RS row. On the next RS row, knit to end. Work 3 more rows even in St st across all sts, working rem wrapped st tog with its wrap when you come to it—26 (30, 34) rows completed; left front measures about 3½ (4, 4½)" (9 [10, 11.5] cm) from CO along selvedge at end of RS rows (lower left front edge). BO all sts.

Sleeves

With smaller needle and RS facing, pick up and knit 90 (94, 106) sts along raglan selvedge between markers (about 4 sts for every 5 rows), then use the cable method (see Glossary, page 131) to CO 3 sts—93 (97, 109) sts total. *Next row:* (WS) P3 (selvedge sts, work in St st throughout), work WS row of broken rib patt (see Stitch Guide) across 90 (94, 106) sts,

then use the cable method to CO 3 sts—96 (100, 112) sts. Work 2 more rows even, keeping 3 sts at each end of needle in St st, and working center sts in broken rib patt. *Dec row:* (RS) K3, ssk, work in patt to last 5 sts, k2tog, k3—2 sts dec'd. Work 3 rows even. Rep the last 4 rows 20 (21, 25) more times—54 (56, 60) sts rem. Work even until sleeve measures about 15½ (16¾, 18)" (39.5 [42.5, 45.5] cm) from pick-up row, ending with a WS row. Cut yarn, leaving a 25½ (27, 28½)" (65 [68.5,

72.5]-cm) tail (about 3 times the width of the edge to be bound off). With tail threaded on a tapestry needle and using the sewn method (see Glossary, page 130), BO all sts in k1, p1 rib. Rep for other sleeve. With yarn threaded on a tapestry needle, sew both sleeve seams.

Waistband

With smaller needle and RS facing, pick up and knit 20 (22, 24) sts along selvedge at lower edge of left front (about 3 sts for every 4

rows), 6 sts across base of sts CO for left sleeve, 98 (110, 122) sts along curved lower back selvedge (about 3 sts for every 4 rows), 6 sts from base of sts CO for right sleeve, and 20 (22, 24) sts along selvedge at lower edge of right front—150 (166, 182) sts total. *Next row:* (WS) P3 (edge sts, work in St st throughout), work WS row of broken rib patt over center 144 (160, 176) sts, p3 (edge sts, work in St st throughout). *RS dec row:* K3, ssk, work in broken rib patt to last 5 sts, k2tog, k3—2 sts dec'd. *WS dec row:* P3, p2tog, work in broken rib patt to last 5 sts, ssp (see Glossary, page 133), p2tog, p3—2 sts dec'd. Rep the last 2 rows 7 more times—118 (134, 150) sts rem; 18 rows completed including pick-up row; waistband measures about 2½" (6.5 cm) high at tallest point.

Edging Short-Rows

K3, sl 1 as if to knit with yarn in back (kwise wyb), k1, pass slipped st over (psso), turn, p3, turn—2 rows worked on first 3 sts only; 1 st joined from live waistband sts. Rep the edging short-rows 111 (127, 143) more times—6 sts rem: 3 sts on right-hand needle that have been used for joining, and 3 sts on left-hand needle. Cut yarn, leaving a 12" (30.5-cm) tail. With yarn threaded on a tapestry needle, graft sts on right-hand needle to sts on left-hand needle (see Glossary, page 134).

Legend

- ☐ knit
- ⦿ yo twice
- ✕ cross-2 (see Stitch Guide)
- ⋒ k1, sl 1, k1 (see Stitch Guide)
- ¤ make hole (see Stitch Guide)
- ▨ no stitch
- ▢ pattern repeat

Lace Ruffle

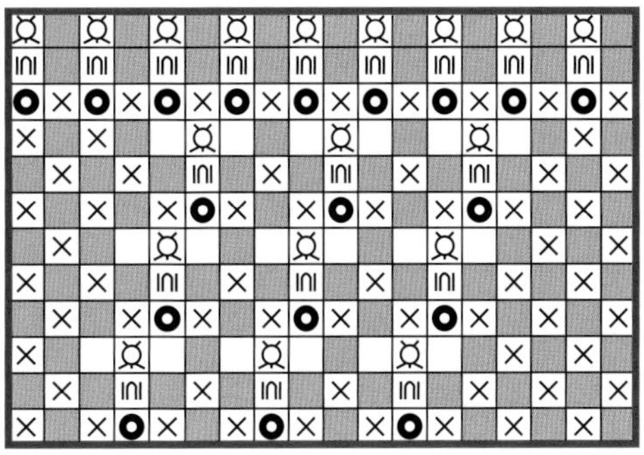

(Lace Ruffle chart, rows 11, 9, 7, 5, 3, 1 numbered at right)

Ruffle

With larger needle, RS facing, and beg at lower edge of right front, pick up and knit 50 (58, 66) sts along CO edge of right front, 14 sts across top of right sleeve, 36 (52, 68) sts across back neck, 14 sts across top of left sleeve, 50 (58, 66) sts along BO edge of left front, and 148 (164, 180) sts across lower edge of waistband (about 1 st for each row)—312 (360, 408) sts total. Place marker (pm) and join for working in the rnd. *Inc rnd:* K1f&b in each of first 10 (0, 4) st(s), *k1f&b in next 9 sts, k1; rep from * 28 (35, 39) more times, k1f&b in next 11 (0, 2) sts, end k1 (0, 2)—594 (684, 774) sts. Place removable marker after every 18 sts if desired (see Notes), so that there are 33 (38, 43) groups of 18 sts. Work Rnd 1 of Lace Ruffle chart. In order to work the alternating cross-2 sts at each end of the rnd properly, it is necessary to reposition the end-of-rnd m as foll:

Before working Rnds 2, 4, 6, 8, and 10: Remove end-of-rnd m, slip last st on right-hand needle (the last st just worked) back onto left-hand needle, replace end-of-rnd m, proceed with rnd as shown on chart; marker has moved 1 st to the right.

Before working Rnds 3, 5, 7, 9, and 11: Remove end-of rnd m, slip first st on left-hand needle onto right-hand needle, replace end-of-rnd m, proceed with rnd as shown on chart; marker has moved 1 st to the left.

It is not necessary to reposition the m before working Rnd 12. When Rnd 12 has been completed, BO all sts loosely.

Finishing

Weave in loose ends. Wash in cold water with mild soap or shampoo and rinse with hair conditioner. Lay flat to dry. When slightly damp, steam-block on WS.

Ribbon Trim

Adjust sewing machine stitch to its longest length and loosen the upper thread tension. Sew two lines of machine stitching 1/4" (6 mm) apart along the center of ribbon. Alternatively, with sewing needle and thread, sew two lines of 1/4" (6-mm) basting or long running stitches in the same manner along center of ribbon. Beg at right shoulder seam, pin centerline of ribbon evenly distributed all the way around the front opening, neck, and lower edge of garment along the pick-up row for the lace ruffle. Pull gently on the basting threads to gather and ruffle the ribbon to fit. With sewing needle and thread, stitch along the centerline of the gathered ribbon as invisibly as possible to secure the ribbon to the pick-up row of lace ruffle. Raw edges at ends of ribbon may be turned under 1/8" (3 mm) and hemmed or trimmed neatly and left unfinished.

Lacy Shawl with Fur Trim

Inspired by a delicate Chancay lace gauze, I asked Sharon Winsauer to design a similar knitted lace pattern for this luxurious Suri alpaca shawl. The lace pattern is worked in a simple rectangle, lined with silk fabric, and trimmed with real Suri fur. I've added four optional mother-of-pearl buttons—cufflink fashion—to the short ends to create "sleeves" so the shawl can be worn as a shrug.

Finished Size 17" (43 cm) wide and 55" (139.5 cm) long, not including fur trim.

Yarn CYCA #1 Super Fine (fingering weight). *Shown here:* The Alpaca Yarn Company Suri Elegance (100% Suri alpaca; 875 yd [800 m]/100 g): #0100 white house (off-white), 1 hank.

Needles Size 6 (4 mm).

Notions Small amount of waste yarn and smooth satin ribbon for provisional cast-on; markers (optional); tapestry needle; 19 by 57" (48.5 by 145 cm) piece of off-white silk charmeuse for lining; 4 yd (3.7 m) Suri alpaca fur ¾" (2 cm) wide (distributed by Lanart); sewing pins; four 1¼" (3.2 cm) buttons (optional); sharp-point sewing needle and matching thread for attaching buttons; sewing machine for attaching fur trim.

Gauge 28 sts and 30½ rows = 4" (10 cm) in Chancay lace patt from chart, after blocking; 1 patt repeat from chart (14 sts and 42 rows)

should block to about 2" (5 cm) wide and 5½" (14 cm) tall. Exact gauge is not critical for this project.

Stitch Guide

Cross-2: (RS and WS rows) K2tog but leave sts on needle, knit both sts tog again through their back loops, then slip both sts from needle. Work very loosely to make it easier to work the cross-2 sts on the following row and to maintain the open, lacy quality of the fabric. The single chart symbol for cross-2 represents 2 sts.

K1, sl 1, k1: (RS and WS rows) K1, sl the yarnover of the previous row as if to knit with yarn in back, k1. If the yarnover is a double yarnover (see chart Rows 13, 16, 19, 34, 37, and 40), drop the extra wrap as you slip the yarnover so only one yarnover loop remains on the needle, leaving an extra-large hole. The single chart symbol for knit 1, slip 1, knit 1 represents 3 sts.

Make hole: (RS and WS rows) Sl the st before the yarnover as if to knit, insert the right needle tip from front to back underneath the slip st strand from the previous row and into the yarnover on the needle, k1 allowing the yo to drop from the needle, pass slipped st over. Insert the right needle tip from front to back into the yarnover hole again to lift the yarnover and slipped st strands onto the right needle, then insert right needle tip into the next st on left needle, k1 from left needle without drawing the new st through the lifted strands, then pass 2 lifted strands on the right needle over the new knit st. The single chart symbol for this represents 3 sts (the slipped yo and 1 st on each side of it) decreased to 2 sts, with a large hole centered below the 2 rem sts. The resulting 2 sts are worked as a cross-2 on the following row.

Notes

- The size of the pattern repeat ranges from 14 to 21 stitches; stitch counts do not remain constant from row to row.
- The gray "no stitch" squares on the chart are placeholders that allow the pattern to line up visually. There is no action associated with them—just skip over the gray squares.
- Some chart symbols represent 2 or 3 stitches; read the Stitch Guide to understand how to work these stitches.
- The double yarnovers in Rows 13, 16, 19, 34, 37, and 40 of the chart create larger-than-usual holes that allow the sides of the piece to remain parallel, counteracting the tendency of the fabric to draw in on these rows.
- If you choose to set off each repeat with markers, be aware that you will have to reposition the markers frequently in order to avoid working a marker into the center of a cross-2, and because adjacent repeats occasionally loan and borrow stitches to and from each other.

Chancay Lace

☐	k on both RS and WS	
2	k2 on both RS and WS	
o	yo	
●	yo twice	
×	cross-2 (see Stitch Guide)	
⋈	k1, sl 1, k1 (see Stitch Guide)	
⍟	make hole (see Stitch Guide)	
▨	no stitch	
☐	pattern repeat	

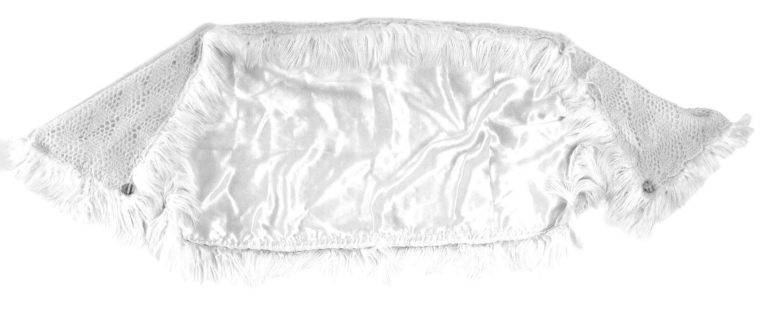

Shawl

With waste yarn and ribbon, and using the ribbon method provisional cast-on (see Glossary, page 131), CO 130 sts. Work Rows 1–42 of Chancay Lace chart a total of 10 times—420 patt rows completed. BO all sts very loosely. Carefully remove waste yarn from base of provisional CO and return sts from base of CO to needle. Rejoin yarn and BO all sts very loosely.

Finishing

Weave in all loose ends.
Wash in cold water with mild soap or shampoo and rinse with hair conditioner. Lay flat to dry. When slightly damp, lightly steam-block on WS.

Lining
Cut lining fabric to measure 19" (48.5 cm) wide and 57" (145 cm) long, or about 2" (5 cm) wider than shawl in each direction. Turn under a 1" (2.5 cm) hem around all 4 edges of lining and sew hem in place by hand or machine. With WS of lining facing upward, use sewing machine to sew alpaca fur along all 4 edges of the lining, being careful to catch as little fur as possible in the stitches. With WS of lining and fur assembly facing up, lay the lace piece on top of lining RS up and pin in place; the right sides of both the lining and lace will face outwards when shawl is worn. With sewing needle and thread, sew lace invisibly to lining around all 4 edges. For an optional shrug effect, make "cuffs" at the short ends as foll: With sewing needle and thread, sew a button to the RS of the lace at each corner, bring the corners of each short end together, and sew through both buttons and all layers of fabric once more to secure the cuff.

Lliclla

Mitered corners redirect the stripes in this shawl inspired by a Chancay tapestry. Nearly every woman in South America uses this type of wrap to hold a baby, firewood, or small parcels. This versatile wrap can be worn a number of ways—folded diagonally lengthwise and draped around the shoulders so that the fold forms a collar; as a rectangular shawl fastened with a pin or brooch in the front, or with one end tossed over the shoulder, or draped over the head like a mantilla and fastened with a pin below the chin.

Finished Size 24" (61 cm) wide and 52" (132 cm) long.

Yarn CYCA #3 Light (DK weight). *Shown here:* The Alpaca Yarn Company Classic Alpaca (100% superfine alpaca; 110 yd [100 m]/ 50 g): #0410 Oregon brown (brown-black) and #2213 cayenne (orange-red), 4 skeins each; #2201 sweet potato (orange) and #2211 mahogany (dark brown), 2 skeins each.

Needles Size 6 (4 mm): 32" (80 cm) circular (cir). Adjust needle size if necessary to obtain the correct gauge.

Notions A few yards of waste yarn for provisional CO; markers (m); tapestry needle.

Gauge 20 sts and 32 rows = 4" (10 cm) in overall pattern st; row gauge is the average gauge taken over St st, garter st, and stranded two-color patterns.

Stitch Guide

Mitered Corner Decreases:

Knit rows: Work to 2 sts before marked corner st, ssk (see Glossary, page 133), slip marker, k1 (corner st), slip marker, k2tog—2 sts dec'd.

Purl rows: Work to 2 sts before marked corner st, p2tog, slip marker, p1 (corner st), slip marker, ssp (see Glossary, page 133)—2 sts dec'd.

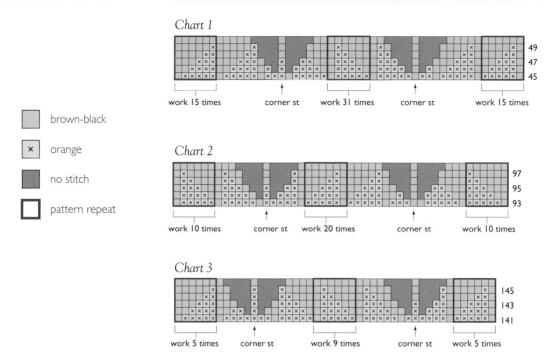

Chart 1

work 15 times   corner st   work 31 times   corner st   work 15 times

49
47
45

Chart 2

work 10 times   corner st   work 20 times   corner st   work 10 times

97
95
93

Chart 3

work 5 times   corner st   work 9 times   corner st   work 5 times

145
143
141

brown-black

× orange

no stitch

pattern repeat

Shawl

With waste yarn and using the provisional method (see Glossary, page 131), CO 128 sts, place marker (pm), CO 1 st (corner st), pm, CO 256 sts, pm, CO 1 st (corner st), pm, CO 128 sts—514 sts total.

Rows 1 and 2: With brown-black, knit 2 rows, working mitered corner decs (see Stitch Guide) on each side of each marked corner st in Row 1 *only*—510 sts rem.

Row 3–6: With orange-red and beg with a RS (knit) row, work in St st for 4 rows, working mitered decs on each side of marked corner sts in first 3 rows—498 sts rem.

Rows 7 and 8: With brown-black, knit 2 rows, working mitered decs in first row *only*—494 sts rem.

Rows 9–12: With dark brown, rep Rows 3–6—482 sts rem.

Rows 13 and 14: With brown-black, rep Rows 7 and 8—478 sts rem.

Rows 15–18: With orange-red, rep Rows 3–6—466 sts rem.

Rows 19 and 20: With brown-black, rep Rows 7 and 8—462 sts rem.

Rows 21–24: With orange, rep Rows 3–6—450 sts rem.

Rows 25 and 26: With brown-black, rep Rows 7 and 8—446 sts rem.

Rows 27–30: With orange-red, rep Rows 3–6—434 sts rem.

Rows 31 and 32: With brown-black, rep Rows 7 and 8—430 sts rem.

Rows 33–36: With dark brown, rep Rows 3–6—418 sts rem.

Rows 37 and 38: With brown-black, rep Rows 7 and 8—414 sts rem.

Rows 39–42: With orange-red, rep Rows 3–6—402 sts rem.

Rows 43 and 44: With brown-black, rep Rows 7 and 8—398 sts rem; 2 marked corner sts, 99 sts in sections at each end of row, 198 sts in center section.

Rows 45–50: With brown-black and orange, work 6 rows of Chart 1, working mitered decs in Rows 46, 47, 48, and 50. Sts dec'd away at corners are indicated by gray "no stitch" areas on chart—382 sts rem.

Rows 51–54: With orange-red, work in St st for 3 rows, beg and ending with a RS knit row, then knit 1 WS row, working mitered decs in first 3 rows—370 sts rem.

Rows 55 and 56: With brown-black, work 2 rows St st, working mitered decs in first row—366 sts rem.

Rows 57–60: With dark brown, rep Rows 51–54—354 sts rem.

Rows 61 and 62: With brown-black, rep Rows 55 and 56—350 sts rem.

Rows 63–66: With orange-red, rep Rows 51–54—338 sts rem.

Rows 67 and 68: With brown-black, rep Rows 55 and 56—334 sts rem.

Rows 69–72: With orange, rep Rows 51–54—322 sts rem.

Rows 73 and 74: With brown-black, rep Rows 55 and 56—318 sts rem.

Rows 75–78: With orange-red, rep Rows 51–54—306 sts rem.

Rows 79 and 80: With brown-black, rep Rows 55 and 56—302 sts rem.

Rows 81–84: With dark brown, rep Rows 51–54—290 sts rem.

Rows 85 and 86: With brown-black, rep Rows 55 and 56—286 sts rem.

Rows 87–90: With orange-red, rep Rows 51–54—274 sts rem.

Rows 91 and 92: With brown-black, rep Rows 55 and 56—270 sts rem; 2 marked corner sts, 67 sts in sections at each end of row, 134 sts in center section.

Rows 93–98: With brown-black and orange, work 6 rows of Chart 2, working mitered decs in Rows 94, 95, 96, and 98, and working Row 98 by knitting all the brown-black sts and purling the orange sts as they appear on the needle—254 sts rem.

Rows 99–102: With orange-red, knit 2 rows, then purl 2 rows, working mitered decs in first 3 rows—242 sts rem.

Rows 103 and 104: With brown-black, work 2 rows St st, working mitered decs in first row—238 sts rem.

Rows 105–108: With dark brown, rep Rows 99–102—226 sts rem.

Rows 109 and 110: With brown-black, rep Rows 103 and 104—222 sts rem.

Rows 111–114: With orange-red, rep Rows 99–102—210 sts rem.

Rows 115 and 116: With brown-black, rep Rows 103 and 104—206 sts rem.

Rows 117–120: With orange, rep Rows 99–102—194 sts rem.

Rows 121 and 122: With brown-black, rep Rows 103 and 104—190 sts rem.

Rows 123–126: With orange-red, rep Rows 99–102—178 sts rem.

Rows 127 and 128: With brown-black, rep Rows 103 and 104—174 sts rem.

Rows 129–132: With dark brown, rep Rows 99–102—162 sts rem.

Rows 133 and 134: With brown-black, rep Rows 103 and 104—158 sts rem.

Rows 135–138: With orange-red, rep Rows 99–102—146 sts rem.

Rows 139 and 140: With brown-black, rep Rows 103 and 104—142 sts rem; 2 marked corner sts, 35 sts in sections at each end of row, 70 sts in center section.

Rows 141–146: With brown-black and orange, work 6 rows of Chart 3, working mitered decs in Rows 142, 143, 144, and 146—126 sts rem.

Rows 147–150: With orange-red, knit 4 rows, working mitered decs in first 3 rows—114 sts rem.

Rows 151 and 152: With brown-black, work 2 rows St st, working mitered decs in first row—110 sts rem.

Rows 153–156: With dark brown, rep Rows 147–150—98 sts rem.

Rows 157 and 158: With brown-black, rep Rows 151 and 152—94 sts rem.

Rows 159–162: With orange-red, rep Rows 147–150—82 sts rem.

Rows 163 and 164: With brown-black, rep Rows 151 and 152—78 sts rem.

Rows 165–168: With orange, rep Rows 147–150—66 sts rem.

Rows 169 and 170: With brown-black, rep Rows 151 and 152—62 sts rem.

Rows 171–174: With orange-red, rep Rows 147–150—50 sts rem.

Rows 175 and 176: With brown-black, rep Rows 151 and 152—46 sts rem.

Rows 177–180: With dark brown, rep Rows 147–150—34 sts rem.

Rows 181 and 182: With brown-black, rep Rows 151 and 152—30 sts rem.

Rows 183–186: With orange-red, rep Rows 147–150—18 sts rem.

Rows 187 and 188: With brown-black, rep Rows 151 and 152—14 sts rem.

Rows 189 and 190: With orange, knit 2 rows, working mitered decs in both rows—6 sts rem; 2 marked corner sts, 1 st in sections at each end of row, 2 sts in center section.

Row 191: With orange, [sl 2 sts as if to k2tog, k1, pass 2 slipped sts over] 2 times, removing markers as you come to them—2 sts rem.

Row 192: With orange, k2tog—1 st rem. Cut yarn, thread tail through rem st, and pull tight to secure.

Finishing

Hem

Carefully remove waste yarn from provisional CO, and place 514 live sts from base of CO on needle; these sts will be from two short sides and one long side of the wrap. With RS facing, join brown-black to *end* of sts on needle. With RS facing, pick up and knit 258 sts along rem long side of wrap (about 4 sts for every 6 rows)—772 sts. Place marker (pm) and join for working in the rnd. *Fold line:* P128, pm, p1 (corner st), pm, p256, pm, p1, pm; rep from * once more, omitting the final marker because end-of-rnd marker is already in place. Knit 3 rnds, working mitered decreases every rnd as foll: *K2tog, knit to 2 sts before next m, ssk, sl m, k1, sl m; rep from * 3 more times—748 sts when all 3 rnds have been completed; 8 sts dec'd each rnd. Knit 1 rnd even. Loosely BO all sts kwise. Fold hem to WS. With brown-black threaded on a tapestry needle, slip-stitch (see Glossary, page 136) hem in place, making sure that the stitching does not show on RS.

Weave in all loose ends.

Wash in cold water with mild soap or shampoo and rinse with hair conditioner. Lay flat to dry. When slightly damp, lightly steam-block on WS.

TRADITIONAL DRESS AND COSTUME

Over the centuries, the Peruvians have developed regional styles of dress that combine the influences of pre-Columbian tradition with the European clothing introduced during the colonial (Spanish) era. Many of these styles remain commonplace in rural Peru, where even everyday clothing reflects regional differences.

Ponchos

The *poncho* dates back to the seventeenth century and apparently is a variation of the *unku* tunic worn by men for centuries. Depending on the region, the ponchos may be woven from alpaca, vicuňa, or cotton. In rainy regions, they can be quite heavy and water repellent. In warmer regions, they can be short and decorative.

Hats

Most traditional Peruvian costumes are capped off by woolen or straw hats, often in bright colors and sometimes highly decorated with embroidery, fringe, or feathers. From the coldest reaches of the Andes we have the *chullo*, a tightly knitted alpaca cap featuring earflaps and colorful geometric motifs. This practical hat, worn only by men in Peru, has become popular in cold regions throughout the world.

Skirts

The traditional Incan *anacu* was transformed by the local women into the brightly colored skirt known as a *pollera*. The skirt is typically black and may be decorated with embroidered flowers or edgings. In many areas, the skirt is worn with a colorful belt and a brightly hued woolen *liclla*. Underneath their skirts, women wear layers of cotton petticoats that may be embroidered.

Dance and Ceremonies

Dances and ceremonies play an important part in Peruvian culture. Many of the costumes worn during these events evolved during the colonial period to include European styles. As with other clothing, the types of costumes vary by region. For the most part, they are brightly colored with embroidery, fringe, feathers, and/or mirrors, and they all include some type of hat.

Carlos Sala/PromPerú

Striped Pullover and Spiral Scarf

Diamond motifs are ubiquitous in pre-Columbian textiles. The version used in this colorful pullover came from a Chancay tapestry and includes a series of graduated pastel stripes accented with duplicate stitches in deeper shades and decorated with bugle beads. Except for the deep neck and overlapping neckband, this pullover follows traditional raglan shaping. The spiral scarf is worked horizontally and shaped by increasing both the number of stitches and needle size.

Finished Size Pullover: 36 (42, 48)" (91.5 [106.5, 122] cm) bust/chest circumference. Scarf: 72" (183 cm) long, measured along shorter cast-on edge.

Yarn CYCA #3 Light (DK weight). *Shown here:* The Alpaca Yarn Company Classic Alpaca (100% superfine alpaca; 110 yd [100 m]/ 50 g): #1414 olive, #1415 sour apple (yellow-green), #1407 araucana (light green-brown), #0206 Waikiki tan (medium brown), #2404 custard (yellow-brown), #0207 Boston beige (light tan), #1632 raindance (denim blue), #1619 blue skies (light gray-blue), #1629 iceberg (pale baby blue), #1818 woodland violet (light violet), #1822 lavender, #1817 purple mist (pale lavender), #2025 confetti (pink-brown heather), #2026 shell (pinkish tan), #2019 petal (pale baby pink), #1405 deep pine (dark green), #2203 fall foliage (red-brown), #1631 blue thunder (dark blue), #1819 Victorian rose (medium pink), and #1800 Ozark purple (dark purple), 1 skein each for all sizes. Leftovers of each color for scarf.

Needles Pullover body and sleeves—size 6 (4 mm): 32" (80 cm) circular (cir). Edging—size 5 (3.75 mm): 32" (80 cm) cir. Scarf—sizes 8 (5 mm), 9 (5.5 mm) and 10 (6 mm): 32" (80 cm) circular (cir) for each size. Adjust needle size if necessary to obtain the correct gauge.

Notions Pullover: Markers (m); tapestry needle; a few yards (meters) of waste yarn and smooth satin ribbon for provisional cast-on; stitch holders; Toho brand Japanese #3 (9 mm) bugle beads (distributed by Bead Station), 1 tube each of colors #617 green matte, #702 deep bronze matte, #611 hematite metallic matte, #705 blue iris matte, and #703 plum iris matte; size 26 tapestry needle or other needle small enough to fit through beads; sewing pins. Scarf: Tapestry needle; 3½ yd (3.2 m) multicolored Offray silk ribbon, optional (available at craft stores).

Gauge Pullover: 21 sts and 27 rows = 4" (10 cm) in St st using larger needles. Adjust needle size if necessary to obtain the correct gauge. Scarf: about 13½ sts and 20 rows = 4" (10 cm) in St st with yarn doubled and using largest needle (exact gauge is not critical for this project).

Notes

- This garment is planned to have a fixed number of rows for the body and sleeves, and the garment pieces are the same length for all sizes. To customize length, work more or fewer rows in the ribbed edgings, adjusting the number and height of stripes as necessary; every 8 rows added or subtracted will lengthen or shorten the piece by about 1" (2.5 cm). Make a note of any changes so you can work the corresponding garment piece to match.
- The back and front are worked separately back and forth in rows to the beginning of the yoke. At the base of the yoke stitches are cast on for each sleeve using a provisional cast-on, and the yoke is worked in the round to the neck. When the yoke has been completed, the sleeves are worked back and forth in rows from the provisional cast-on down to the cuffs.

Front

With smaller needle and dark blue, CO 94 (110, 126) sts. Do not join into a rnd. Working k1, p1 rib back and forth in rows and beg with a RS row, work 2 rows of each color in the foll order: dark blue, denim blue, light gray-blue, pale baby blue, dark purple, light violet, lavender, pale lavender, medium pink, pink-brown heather, pinkish tan, pale baby pink— 24 rows total in rib; piece measures about 2¾" (7 cm) from CO. Change to larger needle. Working St st back and forth in rows and beg with a RS row, work 8 rows of each color in the foll order: olive, yellow-green, light green-brown, medium brown, yellow-brown, light tan, denim blue, light gray-blue—64 rows worked in St st. Change to pale baby blue, work 6 rows even in St st. BO 3 sts at beg of the next 2 rows—88 (104, 120) sts rem; 72 rows total of St st; piece measures about 13½" (34.5 cm) from CO. Place sts on holder.

Back

Work same as front. Leave sts on needle.

Yoke

With waste yarn and ribbon, and using the ribbon method provisional cast-on (see Glossary, page 131), CO 80 (94, 108) sts for left

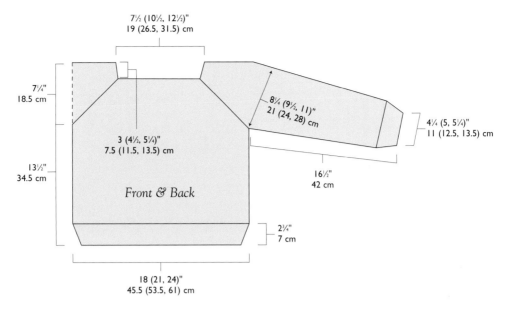

7½ (10½, 12½)"
19 (26.5, 31.5) cm

7¼"
18.5 cm

8¼ (9½, 11)"
21 (24, 28) cm

4¼ (5, 5¼)"
11 (12.5, 13.5) cm

3 (4½, 5¼)"
7.5 (11.5, 13.5) cm

13½"
34.5 cm

Front & Back

2¾"
7 cm

16½"
42 cm

18 (21, 24)"
45.5 (53.5, 61) cm

sleeve at end of back sts already on larger needle, return 88 (104, 120) sts for front to needle with RS facing, then use the ribbon method to CO 80 (94, 108) sts for right sleeve—336 (396, 456) sts total. Join light violet to beg of back sts with RS facing. Knit 1 rnd, placing markers (pm) as foll to mark raglan lines: K88 (104, 120) back sts, pm, k80 (94, 108) left sleeve sts, pm, k88 (104, 120) front sts, pm, k80 (94, 108) right sleeve sts, place different-colored marker to indicate end of rnd. *Dec rnd:* K1, ssk (see Glossary, page 133), *knit to 3 sts before marker (m), k2tog, k1, slip marker (sl m), k1, ssk; rep from * 2 more times, knit to last 3 sts, k2tog, k1—8 sts dec'd. *Note:* Yoke shaping continues throughout color changes for stripes; read the next sections all the way through before proceeding. Work 6 more rnds light violet, then work 8 rnds of each color in the foll order: lavender, pale lavender, pink-brown heather, pinkish tan, pale baby pink—48 rows total in yoke. *At the same time,* after working the first dec rnd, [work 1 rnd even, rep dec rnd] 23 (23, 20) times, then work dec

rnd *every* rnd 0 (0, 6) times—144 (204, 240) sts rem; 40 (56, 66) sts each for front and back, and 32 (46, 54) sts for each sleeve. With pale baby pink, BO all sts.

Sleeves

Carefully remove waste yarn from base of provisional CO of one sleeve, and place 80 (94, 108) live sts onto larger needle. With RS facing, join pale baby blue and use the cable method (see Glossary, page 131) to CO 3 sts at the beg of the next 2 rows—86 (100, 114) sts. *Dec row:* (RS) K2, k2tog, knit to last 4 sts, ssk, k2—2 sts dec'd. *Note:* Sleeve shaping continues throughout color changes for stripes; read the next sections all the way through before proceeding. Work 5 more rows pale baby blue, then work 8 rows of each color in the foll order: light gray-blue, denim blue, light tan, yellow-brown, medium brown, light green-brown, yellow-green, olive, pale baby pink, pinkish tan, pink-brown heather—96 rows total for sleeve. *At the same time,* after working the first dec row, [work 3 rows even, rep dec row] 20 (23, 18) times—44 (52,

76) sts. *For sizes 36 (42)",* sleeve shaping is complete; work even in stripe patt to end. *For size 48",* [work 1 row even, then rep dec row] 10 times, then work even in stripe patt to end—44 (52, 56) sts rem. Change to smaller needle and pale lavender. Knit 1 RS row, then work 1 row k1, p1 rib. Cont in rib, working 2 rows of each color in the foll order: lavender, light violet, pale baby blue, light gray-blue, denim blue, light tan, yellow-brown, medium brown, dark green—20 rows total in rib; cuff measures 2¼" (5.5 cm) from beg of rib; sleeve measures about 16½" (42 cm) total from armhole. With dark green, BO all sts. Work second sleeve in the same manner.

Finishing

Collar

With smaller needles, dark purple, and using the long-tail method (see Glossary, page 131), CO 186 (228, 252) sts. Do not join into a rnd. *Note:* Collar shaping continues throughout color changes for stripes; read the next sections all the way through before proceeding. Working k1, p1 rib back and forth in rows, beg with a RS row

work 2 rows of each color in the foll order: dark purple, pale baby blue, light gray-blue, denim blue, dark blue, light tan, yellow-brown, medium brown, red-brown, light green-brown, yellow-green, olive, dark green—26 rows total in rib. *At the same time,* after working the first 4 rows even in rib, BO 4 sts at beg of next 22 rows—98 (140, 164) sts. Place live sts on a long piece of waste yarn. With center of collar aligned with center back neck, pin last row of collar (with live sts) evenly in place around neck opening, easing in body fullness, and overlapping right front collar over left front, adjusting the amount of overlap to fit. With dark green threaded on a tapestry needle, graft the live sts to the BO edge of neck opening (see Glossary, page 134). Take care to secure every live st, especially where the ends of collar overlap. Conceal loose ends of collar between the two layers of overlapped section. Sew CO edge of right collar to left collar at center front.

Duplicate Stitch Embroidery

With yarn threaded on a tapestry needle, work diagonal lines in duplicate stitch embroidery (see Glossary, page 133) on back and front according to Embroidery and Bead diagram, beg at center of each piece and working toward the edges marked for your size. Work embroidery with colors as foll: dark green on 24 rows of green stripes, red-brown on 24 rows of brown stripes, dark blue on 24 rows of blue stripes, dark purple on 24 rows of purple stripes, and medium pink on 24 rows of pink stripes. Do *not* work any duplicate stitch embroidery on the 4-st raglan welts; this is to help disguise the fact that the embroidery is not continuous around the yoke. *Note:* Although the sleeves were knitted from the top down, work the duplicate stitching in the same direction as for the body so the Vs of the embroidery will be oriented the same way for the entire garment. Work diagonal lines of duplicate stitch embroidery on each sleeve, matching embroidery yarn colors to the stripes in the same manner as for front and back, and beg in the lower center of each sleeve, just above the ribbed cuff. Only the edge sts for the first few rows of sleeve embroidery are marked on diagram; work new sts into embroidery patt as sleeve increases. Again, do not work any embroidery on the 4-st raglan lines at top of sleeves.

Bugle Beads

Separate 20" (51-cm) lengths of dark green, red-brown, dark blue, dark purple, and dark rose into their individual plies. With smaller tapestry needle and using a single ply of same color used for the duplicate stitch embroidery in each stripe, sew pairs of bugle beads in the center of selected diamonds as shown on Embroidery and Bead Diagram, using bead colors as foll: #617 green matte on green stripes, #702 deep bronze matte on brown stripes, #611 hematite metallic matte on blue stripes, #705 blue iris matte on purple stripes, and #703 plum iris matte on pink stripes.

Using yarn tails threaded on a tapestry needle, sew sleeve and side seams and close up small openings at underarms. Weave in loose ends.

Wash in cold water with mild soap or shampoo and rinse with hair conditioner. Lay flat to dry. When slightly damp, block lightly on WS with a steam iron.

Spiral Scarf

Notes

- All colors are used doubled throughout.
- Twist the yarns on the wrong side at color changes, intarsia-style (see Glossary, Page 135), to prevent forming holes, and be consistent in the manner you

clasp the yarns so the finished scarf will have a tidy appearance on the wrong side.

Scarf

With size 8 (5 mm) needle, and using each yarn doubled, CO 10 sts each of 20 colors in the foll order: light baby pink, pinkish tan, pink-brown heather, medium pink, pale lavender, lavender, light violet, dark purple, pale baby blue, light gray-blue, denim blue, dark blue, light tan, yellow-brown, medium brown, red-brown, light green-brown, yellow-green, olive, dark green—200 sts total; when piece is turned to work next row, the dark green sts will be worked first. *Next row:* (WS) Working in colors as they appear, k1f&b (see Glossary, page 135) in each st—400 sts; 20 sts in each color. Work bias stripe patt as foll:

Rows 1 and 3: (RS) With light baby pink k1, ssk, k18 (the intarsia pattern moves 1 st to the left), *k20 with the next color; rep from * 18 more times, with dark green k17, k1f&b, k1.

Rows 2 and 4: (WS) Purl, working colors as they appear.

Change to size 9 (5.5 mm) needle and work Rows 1–4, Change to size 10 (6 mm) needle and work Rows 1–4 of patt, then work Rows 1 and 2 once more—piece measures about 2½" (6.5 cm) from CO, measured straight up along a single column

of sts. Loosely BO all sts in colors as they appear.

Finishing

Weave in all loose ends. Wash in cold water with mild soap or shampoo and rinse with hair conditioner. Lay flat to dry. When slightly damp, lightly steam-block on WS.

Ribbon Trim

(optional) With silk ribbon threaded on a tapestry needle, work whipstitch (see Glossary, page 136) along entire CO edge. Hold one end of scarf high above your head and use the other hand to gently coax the ruffled fabric into even spirals with the purl side facing outward for an exaggerated ruffle look.

Embroidery and Bead Diagram

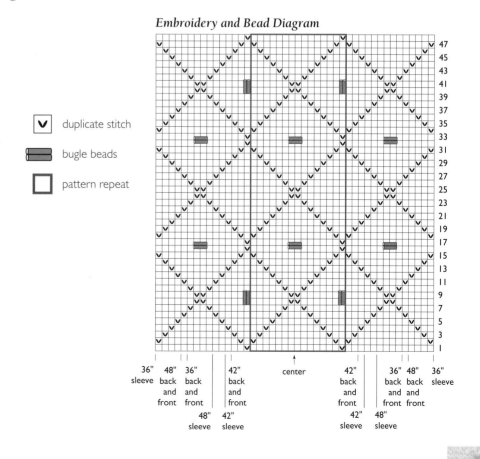

∨ duplicate stitch

▬ bugle beads

□ pattern repeat

Short Circular Cardigan

T his unusual cardigan, worked in two pieces, incorporates the pattern of a Chancay tapestry dating from around A.D. 1100 to 1470. The piece that forms the sleeves and upper body is worked first from cuff to cuff in royal blue and parrot green in the Fair Isle stranded color-work technique. The collar, lower back, and fronts are picked up and worked lengthwise from this piece in a ribbed pattern shaped with short-rows to produce a flowing silhouette. For an added detail, parrot green I-cord outlines the shoulder and sleeve seams.

Finished Size 36 (43)" (91.5 [109] cm) bust circumference. Sweater shown measures 36" (91.5 cm). *Note:* Amount of overlap at front can be adjusted to accommodate a slightly smaller or larger bust size.

Yarn CYCA #3 Light (DK weight). *Shown here:* The Alpaca Yarn Company Classic Alpaca (100% superfine alpaca, 110 yd [100 m]/50 g): #1627 royal, 10 (12) skeins.

CYCA #3 Light (DK weight). *Shown here:* Alpaca with a Twist Baby Twist (100% baby alpaca; 110 yd [100 m]/50 g): #4003 Polly parrot green, 4 (6) skeins.

Needles Body and sleeves—size 7 (4.5 mm): 32" (60 cm) circular (cir). Edging—size 6 (4 mm): 32" (60-cm) cir and set of 2 double-pointed (dpn) for I-cord trim. Adjust needle size if necessary to obtain the correct gauge.

Notions Removable markers (m) or safety pins; stitch holders; tapestry needle; small amount of waste yarn and smooth satin ribbon for provisional cast-on.

Gauge 19½ sts and 22 rows = 4" (10 cm) in St st color work from charts using larger needle; 20½ sts and 23 rows = 4" (10 cm) in solid-color St st using smaller needle.

Stitch Guide

Sleeve increases: At the beginning of a RS row, work k2, k1f&b; at the end of a RS row, work in patt to last 3 sts, k1f&b, k2.

Sleeve decreases: At the beginning of a RS row, work k2, ssk; at the end of a RS row, work in patt to last 4 sts, k2tog, k2.

- The sleeve seams run along the top of each arm, from base of neck and over the shoulder to cuff.
- The "wingspan" of this garment is planned to be 57 (60½)" (145 [153.5] cm) from cuff to cuff, with no allowance for adjusting sleeve length.
- Charts are worked in stranded stockinette stitch. Use a single strand of each color all the way across from selvedge to selvedge, and catch the long floats on the wrong side every 2 to 3 stitches by twisting the yarns together to prevent the strands from being snagged when the garment is worn.
- When working short-rows in color-work pattern from charts, wrap stitches with the color that matches the stitch being wrapped.

Sleeves and Upper Back

Left Sleeve

With smaller needle and royal, CO 50 (58) sts. Beg and ending with a RS row, work in St st for 9 rows for cuff facing, dec 1 st at each end of needle (see Stitch Guide) on the 3rd and 7th rows— 46 (54) sts; facing measures about 1¾" (4.5 cm) from CO. Knit 1 WS row for fold line. Change to larger needle. Work in patt from Left

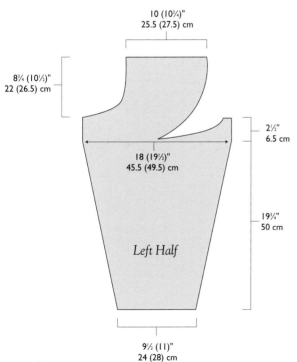

10 (10¾)"
25.5 (27.5) cm

8¾ (10½)"
22 (26.5) cm

2½"
6.5 cm

18 (19½)"
45.5 (49.5) cm

19¾"
50 cm

Left Half

9½ (11)"
24 (28) cm

Half chart (see page 94; smaller size is shown outlined in red), and *at the same time* inc 1 st (see Stitch Guide) at each end of needle on Row 3 of chart, work 3 rows even, then beg with Row 7 of chart, *inc 1 st each end of next RS row, work 5 rows even, inc 1 st each end of foll RS row, work 3 rows even (4 sts inc'd in 10 rows); rep from * 8 more times, [inc 1 st each end of next RS row, work 5 rows even] 2 times to end Row 108 of chart— 88 (96) sts; piece measures about 19¾" (50 cm) from fold line. Mark both ends of last row completed with removable markers or waste yarn to indicate end of left sleeve. With RS facing, place last 44 (48) sts of row on holder—44 (48) sts rem.

Left Front Extension

Working back and forth in rows on rem 44 (48) sts, cont in patt from chart, shaping left front extension using short-rows (see Glossary, page 136) as foll (wrapped sts are not shown on chart):

Row 109 of chart: (RS) Work in patt to last 4 sts, wrap next st, turn.

Even-numbered Rows 110–120: Work in patt to end.

Rows 111, 113, and 115: Work in patt to 8 sts before previously wrapped st, wrap next st, turn.

Row 117: Work in patt to 4 (8) sts before previously wrapped st, wrap next st, turn.

Rows 119 and 121: Work in patt to 4 sts before previously wrapped st, wrap next st, turn.

Row 122: Work in patt to end; piece measures about 2½" (6.5 cm) from dividing row, measured straight up along a single column of sts at tallest point.

With royal, knit 1 RS row across all sts, working wrapped sts tog with their wraps as you come to them. Place 44 (48) sts on holder or waste yarn.

Left Back

Return 44 (48) held sts to larger needle and join yarns with RS facing. Resume working patt from chart beg with Row 109. *Note:* The edges of the piece have different shaping; read the next section all the way through before proceeding. Inc 1 st at end of row on Rows

109, 113, and 117, and *at the same time,* beg with Row 109, use the cable method (see Glossary, page 131) to CO 2 sts at beg of next 6 RS rows (Row 109 through Row 119, inclusive)—59 (63 sts); Row 119 of chart completed. Cont in patt from chart, BO 2 sts at beg of next 11 WS rows (Row 120 to Row 140), then BO 1 st at beg of foll WS row, and *at the same time* use the cable method to CO 2 sts at beg of RS Rows 123, 127, 131, 135, 139, and 147—48 (52) sts; Row 147 of chart completed. Work even until Row 157 (167) of chart has been completed—piece measures about 28½ (30¼)" (72.5 [77] cm) from fold line at cuff. Mark both ends of last row completed with removable markers or scrap yarn to indicate centerline of back.

Right Back

Cont in patt on 48 (52) sts from Right Half chart (see page 95), beg with Row 178 (168) as indicated for your size (smaller size is outlined in red); because the Left Half chart ended at the centerline on a RS row, the first row shown on Right Half chart is a WS row. *Note:* The edges of the piece have different shaping; read the next section all the way through before proceeding. BO 2 sts at beg of RS Rows 189 and 197, then BO 2 sts at beg of every other RS row 5 times (Rows 201 through 217). *At the same time,* inc 1 st at end of

Row 193, then use the cable method to CO 2 sts at beg of the next 11 WS rows (Row 196 through 216)—57 (61) sts rem when Row 217 has been completed. BO 2 sts at beg of the next 5 RS rows (Row 219 through Row 227). *At the same time,* dec 1 st at end of Rows 219, 223, and 227—44 (48) sts rem. Place sts on holder.

Right Front Extension

With larger needle, waste yarn and ribbon, and using the ribbon method provisional cast-on (see Glossary, page 131), CO 44 (48) sts. Join royal with WS facing and purl 1 WS row. Work in patt from Right Half chart, shaping right front extension using short-rows as foll (wrapped sts are not shown on chart):

Row 213 of chart: (RS) Work in patt for 4 sts, wrap next st, turn.

Even-numbered Rows 214–226: Work in patt to end.

Rows 215 and 217: Work in patt to wrapped st, work wrapped st tog with its wrap, work 3 sts in patt, wrap next st, turn.

Row 219: Work in patt to wrapped st, work wrapped st tog with its wrap, work 3 (7) sts in patt, wrap next st, turn.

Rows 221, 223, and 225: Work in patt to wrapped st, work wrapped st tog with its wrap, work 7 sts in patt, wrap next st, turn.

Row 227: Work in patt to end,

working rem wrapped st tog with its wrap as you come to it. Break yarns.

Right Sleeve

Return 44 (48) held sts of right back to larger needle so that when RS is facing the back sts are the second group of sts on the needle—88 (96) sts. With WS facing, rejoin yarns and work WS row 228 of chart across all sts. Mark both ends of last row completed with removable markers or waste yarn to indicate beg of right sleeve. Beg with RS Row 233, shape sleeve as foll: *dec 1 st each end of next RS row, work 5 rows even, dec 1 st each end of foll RS row, work 3 rows even (4 sts dec'd in 10 rows); rep from * 9 more times, then dec 1 st at each end of foll RS row—46 (54) sts rem. Work Row 334 of chart even—piece measures about 57 (60½)" (145 [153.5] cm) from fold line for left sleeve cuff; 314

Left Half

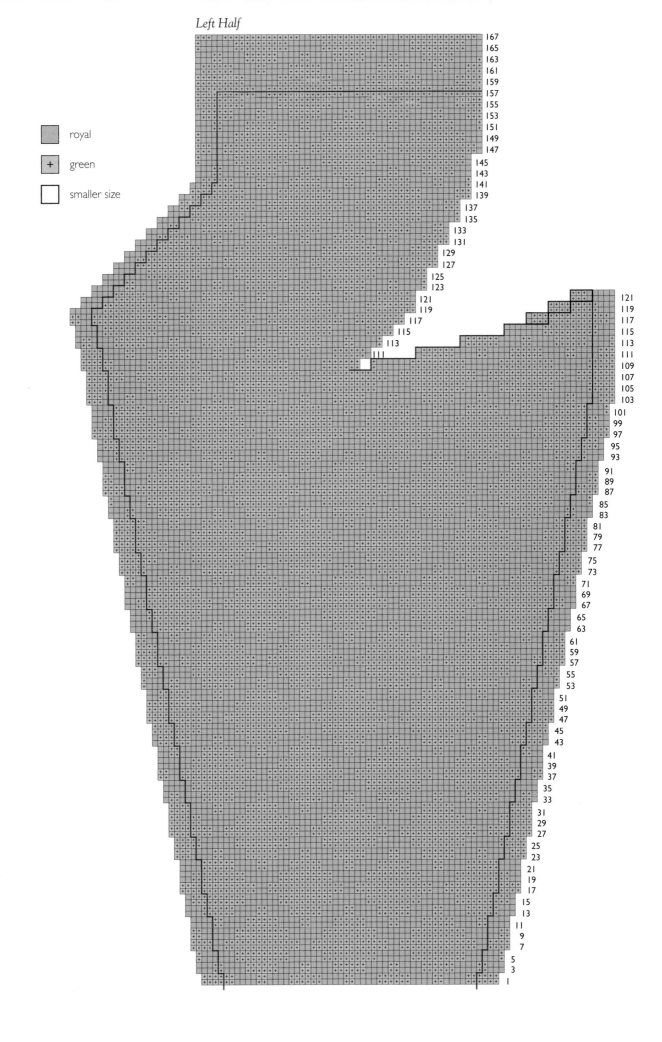

royal

+ green

smaller size

167
165
163
161
159
157
155
153
151
149
147
145
143
141
139
137
135
133
131
129
127
125
123
121
119
117
115
113
111

121
119
117
115
113
111
109
107
105
103
101
99
97
95
93
91
89
87
85
83
81
79
77
75
73
71
69
67
65
63
61
59
57
55
53
51
49
47
45
43
41
39
37
35
33
31
29
27
25
23
21
19
17
15
13
11
9
7
5
3
1

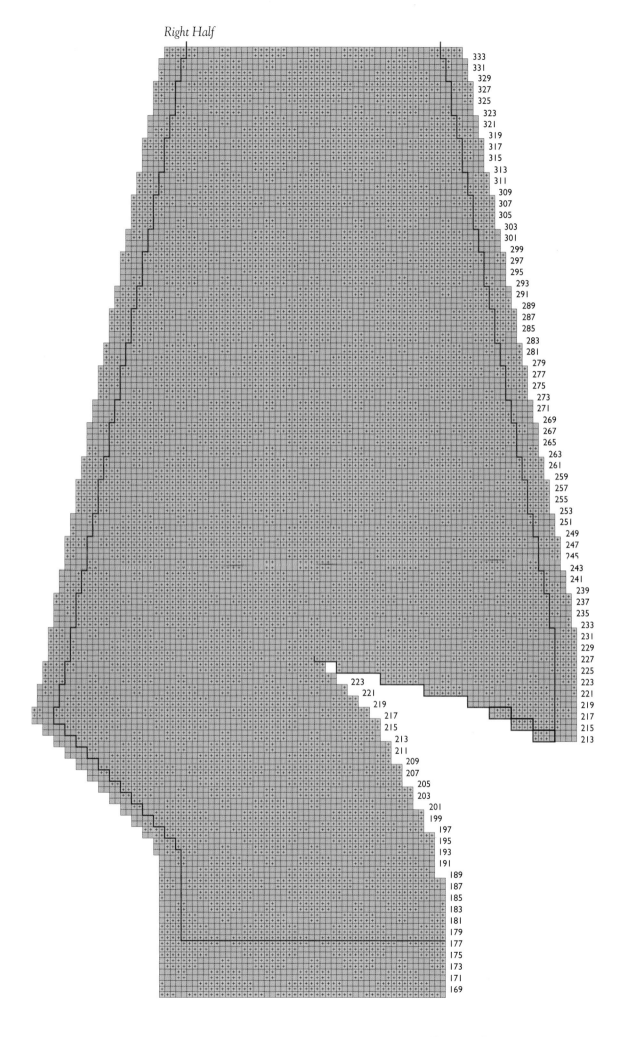

Right Half

333
331
329
327
325
323
321
319
317
315
313
311
309
307
305
303
301
299
297
295
293
291
289
287
285
283
281
279
277
275
273
271
269
267
265
263
261
259
257
255
253
251
249
247
245
243
241
239
237
235
233
231
229
227
225
223
221
219
217
215
213

223
221
219
217
215
213
211
209
207
205
203
201
199
197
195
193
191
189
187
185
183
181
179
177
175
173
171
169

(334) rows total completed from charts; smaller size uses 10 fewer rows from each chart. Change to smaller needle. With royal, purl 1 RS row for fold line. Change to smaller needle. Work even in St st for 9 rows, beg and ending with a WS row, and inc 1 st at each end of needle on 2nd and 8th rows—50 (58) sts rem. BO all sts.

Edging

With royal threaded on a tapestry needle, sew sleeve seams along tops of arms, easing front extensions to fit. With smaller needle, royal, RS facing, and beg at top of right sleeve seam, pick up and knit 57 (72) sts across back neck to top of left sleeve seam (about 3 sts for every 4 rows), return 44 (48) held sts of left front extension to left-hand needle with RS facing and knit across sts of left front extension, pick up and knit 74 (89) sts across lower back edge (about 3 sts for every 4 rows), carefully remove waste yarn and ribbon from base of provisional CO of right front extension and place 44 (48) sts of right front extension on left-hand needle with RS facing, and knit across sts of right front extension, finishing where you began at top of right sleeve seam—219 (257) sts total. Join for working in the rnd, and place marker (pm) for beg of rnd. *Next rnd:* *P3, p2tog; rep from * to last 4 (2) sts, p4 (2)—176 (206) sts rem. Break yarn. Place additional markers (m) or safety pins on needle as foll: 1 in the center of lower

back (or as close to center as possible), then place m at fold of each sleeve at what would be the base of the armholes if the garment had conventional armholes—2 marked lower back sections. Place 2 more m in each marked section to divide it as evenly as possible into 3 equal parts, adjusting the position of the outermost markers inward or outward as necessary—7 lower back markers total; 6 marked sections centered on the lower back with an equal number of sts in each section. Place 1 more marker at top of left sleeve seam—this marker and end-of-rnd marker indicate the sts of the back neck. With RS facing, and using the ribbon method provisional cast-on, CO 50 sts onto end of right-hand needle.

Right Front

With WS facing, rejoin royal. Work the basic edging patt back and forth on 50 newly CO sts using short-rows and joining to the body as foll:

Set-up row: (WS) P20, [k4, p9] 2 times, k3, slip (sl) 1 st as if to knit (kwise), k1 body st, pass slipped st over (psso), turn.

Row 1: (RS) Sl 1 as if to purl (pwise), p3, [k9, p4] 2 times, k20.

Row 2: (WS short-row) P20, wrap next st, turn.

Row 3: (RS short-row) K20 to end.

Row 4: P20, [k4, p9] 2 times, working wrapped st tog with its wrap when you come to it, k3, sl 1 kwise, k1 body st, psso—1

st joined from body at end of row.

Row 5: Sl 1 pwise, p3, [k9, p4] 2 times, p20.

Row 6: K20, wrap next st, turn.

Row 7: P20 to end.

Row 8: K20, [p4, k9] 2 times working wrapped st tog with its wrap when you come to it, k3, sl 1 kwise, k1 body st, psso—1 st joined from body at end of row.

Rep Rows 1–8 for basic edging patt (do *not* rep the set-up row), along right front extension, joining 2 sts from body for every 8 edging rows, until you reach the first m at base of right armhole.

Lower Back

If necessary, work more rows to end with a WS row having just completed a 4-row stripe of either St st or rev St st at outer selvedge. The lower back edging introduces extra short-rows to the basic edging patt to flare out the lower back, peplum-style. Work the extra short-rows for the lower back as foll, maintaining alternate 4-row stripes of St st or rev St st at outer selvedge of edging as established:

Row 1: (RS) Sl 1 pwise, p3, [k9, p4] 2 times, work last 20 sts as either k20 or p20 to maintain patt.

Row 2: Work 20 sts in patt, wrap next st, turn.

Row 3: Work 20 sts in patt to end.

Row 4: Work 20 sts in patt, knit wrapped st tog with its wrap, k3, wrap next st, turn.

Row 5: Sl 1 pwise, p3, work 20 sts in patt to end.

Rows 6 and 7: Rep Rows 2 and 3.

Row 8: Work 20 sts in patt, k4, purl wrapped st tog with its wrap, p8, wrap next st, turn.

Row 9: Sl 1 pwise, k8, p4, work 20 sts in patt to end.

Rows 10 and 11: Rep Rows 2 and 3.

Row 12: Work 20 sts in patt, k4, p9, knit wrapped st tog with its wrap, k3, wrap next st, turn.

Row 13: Sl 1 pwise, p3, k9, p4, work 20 sts in patt.

Rows 14 and 15: Rep Rows 2 and 3.

Row 16: Work 20 sts in patt, k4, p9, k4, purl wrapped st tog with its wrap, p8, wrap next st, turn.

Row 17: Sl 1 pwise, k8, p4, k9, p4, work 20 sts in patt.

Rows 18 and 19: Rep Rows 2 and 3.

Row 20: Work 20 sts in patt, [k4, p9] 2 times, knit wrapped st tog with its wrap, k2, sl 1 kwise, k1 body st, psso—1 st joined from body at end of row.

Resume working basic 8-row edging patt as for right front, continuing to alternate 4-row stripes of St st and rev St st at outer selvedge (which may require diverging from the exact 8-row patt originally given), until you reach the next lower back m. If necessary, complete the 4-row stripe you are on, then work Rows 1–20 of lower back short-row patt again. Cont in this manner, working the basic edging patt until you reach a marker, then working the 20-row lower back short-row sequence at the marker, until you have worked the 20-row lower back short-row sequence at each of the 7 lower back markers.

Left Front

Resume working 8-row basic edging patt as for right front, continuing to alternate 4-row stripes of St st and rev St st at outer selvedge, until you reach the marker at top of left sleeve seam.

Back Neck

If necessary, work more rows to end with a WS row having just completed a 4-row stripe. Cont across the back neck, joining 2 body sts for every WS edging row, and discontinuing the short-rows for the 4-row stripe patt as foll:

Rows 1 and 3: (RS) Sl 1 pwise, p3, [k9, p4] 2 times, work 20 sts in patt.

Rows 2 and 4: Work 20 sts in patt, [k4, p9] 2 times, k3, sl 1 kwise, k2tog (next 2 body sts), psso—2 sts joined from body at end of row.

Rep these 4 rows for patt, maintaining 4-rows stripes of St st and rev St st as established, until about 10–12 body sts rem to be joined. In order for the edging patt to be continuous when the two ends are grafted tog, the edging must end with a complete 4-row stripe in rev St st. Every 4-row stripe uses up 2 sts from the body, so count ahead to see if there are enough body sts left to end with a 4-row rev St st stripe. If not, "fudge" the pattern by working an occasional WS row that joins only 1 body st (to slow down the rate at which the body sts are used up) as foll: Work 20 sts in patt, [k4, p9] 2 times, k3, sl 1 kwise, k1 (next body st), psso—1 st joined from body at end of row. When all body sts have been joined, carefully remove waste yarn and ribbon from base of provisional CO for edging and place sts from base of CO on other end of cir needle or dpn. With yarn threaded on a tapestry needle, graft live edging sts to sts from base of CO (see Glossary, page 134).

Finishing

Fold cuff facings to WS along fold lines and sew invisibly in place. Weave in loose ends.

I-cord Sleeve Trim

(make 2) With parrot and dpn, CO 3 sts. Work 3-st I-cord (see Glossary, page 135) until piece measures about 21¾" (55 cm), slightly stretched, to fit the length of the sleeve seam. BO all sts. With parrot threaded on a tapestry needle, sew I-cord to sleeve, covering sleeve seam.

Wash in cold water with mild soap or shampoo and rinse with hair conditioner. Lay flat to dry. When slightly damp, lightly steam-block sleeves and back on WS; avoid steaming the ridges along the outer rim of the edging to prevent flattening them so they maintain their "corrugated" appearance.

Circular Cardigan with Tapestry Weaving

M any pre-Columbian textiles are decorated with embroidery. I incorporated the intertwined motif from a Chancay tapestry into a decorative band around the edge of this long open cardigan. The body of this garment is worked in one piece from cuff to cuff in a lightly textured stitch pattern. The band is worked separately in stockinette stitch, then embroidered before being sewn to the body, with a self facing that folds to the inside and adds stability. The drapey sideways-knit body combined with the firm embroidered band allows the garment to flow gracefully at the back and hug the body nicely in the front.

Finished Size 40 (45, 51)" (101.5 [114.5, 129.5] cm) bust circumference. Shown in size 45" (114.5 cm). *Note:* Front edges of cardigan deliberately do not meet at center front.

Yarn CYCA #3 Light (DK weight). *Shown here:* The Alpaca Yarn Company Classic Alpaca (100% superfine alpaca; 110 yd [100 m]/50 g): #2000 California claret (MC, red), 14 (15, 17) skeins; #2213 cayenne (orange-red), #2201 sweet potato (orange), #1810 purple mountain majesty, #1411 green tea (dark olive), and #2211 mahogany (dark brown), 1 skein each for woven embroidery.

Needles Body, sleeves, and embroidered band—size 7 (4.5 mm): 32" (60 cm) circular (cir). Cuff facings and band grafting—size 6 (4 mm): 32" (60 cm) cir and 2 double-pointed (dpn). Adjust needle size if necessary to obtain the correct gauge.

Notions A few yards (meters) of waste yarn and smooth satin ribbon for provisional cast-on; markers (m); stitch holders; tapestry needle; sewing pins.

Gauge 21 sts and 29 rows = 4" (10 cm) in dot stitch patt using larger needle.

Stitch Guide

Dot Stitch: (multiple of 2 sts)
Rows 1 and 3: (RS) Knit.
Row 2: *K1, p1; rep from *.
Row 4: *P1, k1; rep from *.
Repeat Rows 1–4 for pattern.

Sleeve increases: At the beginning of a RS row, work k2, k1f&b; at the end of a RS row, work in patt to last 3 sts, k1f&b, k2.

Sleeve decreases: At the beginning of a RS row, work k2, ssk; at the end of a RS row, work in patt to last 4 sts, k2tog, k2.

- The body of this garment is worked in one piece from cuff to cuff. The band is sewn around the entire front opening after the woven embroidery is completed.
- The "wingspan" of this garment is planned to be 57½ (60, 63)" (146 [152.5, 160] cm). To customize sleeve length, work more or fewer rows at the top of each sleeve; every 6 rows added or subtracted will lengthen or shorten the sleeve by about ¾" (2 cm). Make a note of any changes so you can work the second sleeve to match.
- The weight of the band and sideways direction of knitting will cause the garment to grow about 1–2" (2.5–5 cm) in length when worn.

Left Sleeve

Cuff Facing

With MC and smaller cir needle, CO 44 (46, 48) sts. Do not join. Working back and forth in rows, work St st for 10 rows, beg with a WS row and dec 1 st at each end of needle on the 2nd and 6th rows (see Stitch Guide)—40 (42, 44) sts rem. Knit 1 WS row for fold line. Change to larger cir needle. Keeping 2 sts at each side in St st to end of sleeve, work dot stitch (see Stitch Guide) over center 36 (38, 40) sts and inc for sleeve as foll: *Inc 1 st at each end of needle on next RS row, work 3 rows even, inc 1 st at each end of needle on foll RS row, work 5 rows even; rep from * 11 (12, 11) more times, working inc'd sts into patt—88 (94, 92) sts.

Sizes 40 (45)" Only

Inc 1 st at each end of needle on next RS row—90 (96) sts; sleeve measures about 16¾ (18)" (42.5 [45.5] cm) from fold line.

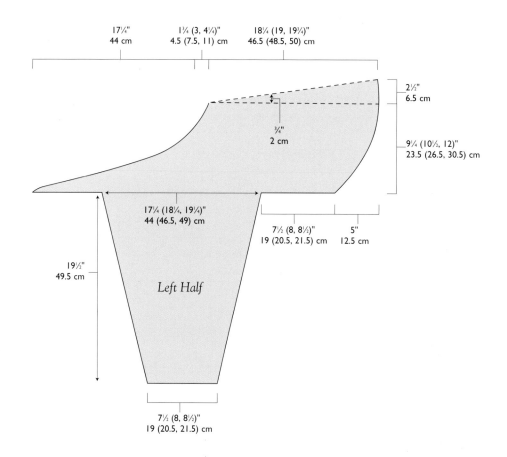

Size 51" Only

Inc 1 st at each end of next RS row, work 1 row even; rep the last 2 rows 4 more times—(102) sts; sleeve measures about 18" (45.5 cm) from fold line.

All Sizes

Work even in dot stitch until sleeve measures 19½" (49.5 cm) from fold line, or desired length (see Notes), ending with a WS row.

Left Front and Back

With waste yarn and ribbon, and using the ribbon method provisional cast-on (see Glossary, page 131), CO 40 (42, 44) sts at beg of needle, work 1 RS row in patt across 90 (96, 102) sleeve sts, use the ribbon provisional method to CO 40 (42, 44) more sts—170 (180, 190) sts. Work 1 WS row across all sts, working newly CO sts into established patt. *Note:* Cutaway edge of left front is shaped at same time as curved edge of lower back; read the next sections all the way through before proceeding.

Shape Front

At beg of WS rows, BO 2 sts 2 times, then BO 4 sts 7 times, then BO 6 sts 2 times, then BO 8 sts 2 times, then BO 10 sts 3 times—90 sts total BO along left front edge; 33 rows completed from end of sleeve, including first WS body row. *At the same time*, shape left lower back as foll:

Shape Lower Back

At beg of RS rows, use the cable method (see Glossary, page 131) to CO 2 sts 8 times, then inc 1 st at beg of row as for sleeve every other row 6 times, then every 4 rows once, ending with a WS row—23 sts inc'd at beg of RS rows for lower back edge; 33 rows completed from end of sleeve, including first WS body row. After completing these shaping instructions there will be 103 (113, 123) sts; piece measures about 4½" (11.5 cm) from provisional CO.

Shape Back Neck

(work at same time as shaping lower back) At end of RS rows (neck edge), dec 1 st as for sleeve every other row 6 (12, 18) times, then every 4 rows 2 (2, 3) times, then every 6 rows 1 (2, 1) time(s), then every 8 rows 1 (0, 0) time— 10 (16, 22) sts dec'd at neck edge; 34 (44, 54) rows in neck shaping. *At the same time,* cont left lower back shaping as foll: At lower back edge (beg of RS rows) inc 1 st every 6 rows once, then every 8 rows once, then every 10 rows once, then work even at lower back edge until left back neck shaping has been completed—3 more sts inc'd at lower back edge. After completing these shaping instructions there will be 96 (100, 104) sts; piece measures about 9¼ (10½, 12)" (23.5 [26.5, 30.5] cm) from provisional CO.

Short-rowed Center Back Panel

Cont in patt, working short-rows (see Glossary, page 136) as foll:

Row 1: (RS) Work in patt to last 20 sts, wrap next st, turn.

Even-numbered Rows 2–8: Work in patt to end.

Odd-numbered Rows 3–7: Work in patt to 19 (20, 21) sts before previous wrapped st, wrap next st, turn.

Row 9: Work in patt to end, working wrapped sts tog with their wraps as you come to them.

Row 10: Work in patt to end.

Row 11: Work 19 (20, 21) sts in patt, wrap next st, turn.

Even-numbered Rows 12–16: Work in patt to end.

Odd-numbered Rows 13 and 15: Work in patt to wrapped st, work wrapped st tog with its wrap, work 19 (20, 21) sts in patt, wrap next st, turn.

Row 17: Work in patt to wrapped st, work wrapped st tog with its wrap, work to last 20 sts, wrap next st, turn.

Row 18: Work in patt to end.

Right Front and Back

Work 1 RS row in patt across all sts, working rem wrapped st tog with its wrap when you come to it, then work 1 WS row even—still 96 (100, 104) sts. *Note:* As for left front and back, shaping takes place along both edges at the same time; read the next sections all the way through before proceeding.

Shape Back Neck

(work at same time as shaping lower back) At end of RS rows (neck edge), inc 1 st as for sleeve every 8 rows 1 (0, 0) time, then every 6 rows 1 (2, 1) time(s), then every 4 rows 2 (2, 3) times, then

every other row 6 (12, 18) times—10 (16, 22) sts inc'd at neck edge; 34 (44, 54) rows in neck shaping. *At the same time,* shape lower back as foll:

Shape Lower Back

At lower back edge (beg of RS rows), work 10 (20, 30) rows even, then dec 1 st as for sleeves every 10 rows once, then every 8 rows once, then every 6 rows once—3 sts dec'd at lower back edge. After completing these shaping instructions there will be 103 (113, 123) sts.

Shape Right Front

(work at same time as shaping lower right back) At beg of WS rows use the cable method to CO 10 sts 3 times, then CO 8 sts 2 times, then CO 6 sts 2 times, then CO 4 sts 7 times, then CO 2 sts 2 times—90 sts total CO along right front edge; 32 rows in right front shaping. *At the same time,* cont lower back shaping as foll: At beg of RS rows, dec 1 st as for sleeve every 4 rows once, then every other row 6 times, then BO 2 sts 8 times—23 sts dec'd or BO for lower back edge; 32 rows in this section of lower back shaping. After completing these shaping instructions there will be 170 (180, 190) sts. Place 40 (42, 44) sts at each end of needle on separate holders or waste yarn to be joined later for right side seam—90 (96, 102) center sts for sleeve rem.

Right Sleeve

Keeping 2 sts at each edge in St st as for left sleeve, work even in patt until sleeve measures 2¾ (1¼,

1½)" (7 [3.2, 3.8] cm) from where sts were put on hold for right side, ending with a WS row.

Sizes 40 (45)" Only

Dec 1 st at each end of needle on next RS row, then work 1 row even—88 (94) sts rem.

Size 51" Only

Dec 1 st at each end of next RS row, work 1 row even; rep the last 2 rows 4 more times—(92) sts rem.

All Sizes

*Dec 1 st at each end of needle on next RS row, work 5 rows even, dec 1 st at each end of needle on foll RS row, work 3 rows even; rep from * 11 (12, 11) more times—40 (42, 44) sts rem; right sleeve should measure about 19½" (49.5 cm), or same length as left sleeve to fold line. Change to smaller cir needle. Purl 1 RS row for fold line. Work in St st for 10 rows, beg with a WS row, and inc 1 st at each end of needle on the 4th and 8th rows—44 (46, 48) sts. BO all sts.

Circular Band

Join Side Seams

Carefully remove waste yarn from provisional CO sts of right side seam and place sts on separate needles. With MC threaded on a tapestry needle, graft front to back at right side seam (see Glossary, page 134). Rep for left side seam.

Band

With larger cir needle, waste yarn and ribbon, use the ribbon

- ■ dark brown
- ▨ dark olive
- ■ orange-red
- ▨ purple
- □ orange

Woven Embroidery

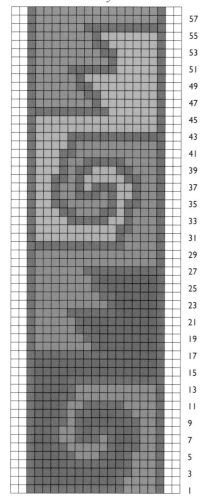

method provisional cast-on to CO 43 sts. Work band patt as foll:

Row 1: (RS) K43.

Row 2: (WS) P22, slip 1 st as if to purl with yarn in front for fold line, p22.

Rep Rows 1 and 2 until band fits around the entire front opening. *Note:* The total number of band rows must be divisible by 29 to match the outline of the stepped fret motifs, or divisible by 58 to match both the motifs and the color placement, when the band is sewn into a circle—band shown has 464 rows to accommodate 8 full 58-row reps of embroidery. When band has been completed, place sts on holder or waste yarn until embroidery is finished.

Embroidery

Embroidery is worked over 21 sts from right half of band with RS facing. The left half of the band will be folded to the WS along the column of slipped sts to form a facing when garment is finished. With 2 strands of dark brown threaded on a tapestry needle and RS facing, use a backstitch (see Glossary, page 133) to embroider 2 vertical lines the length of the band as shown on Woven Embroidery chart, with 1 line of stitching covering the third column of sts from the band selvedge, and the other covering the fourth column of sts from the column of slipped sts—15 sts rem between embroidered st columns. With 2 strands of dark brown threaded on a tap-

estry needle, use a backstitch to outline the stepped fret motifs shown on chart, covering an entire knitted st with each backstitch. Fill the stepped fret motifs with woven stitch embroidery (see Glossary, page 134) using single strands of dark olive, orange-red, purple, and orange as shown on chart. With dark olive and working according to Row 1 of chart, weave the yarn across the first row of knitting from right to left, working over half a knit st, then under half a knit st, for every dark olive square in Row 1, then reverse direction and weave across the same sts, alternating the manner in which you weave over and under half of each st. With orange-red threaded on a tapestry needle, embroider the orange-red squares of Row 2 in the same manner. Changing colors as needed and filling in one chart row at a time with each color, work until Row 58 of chart has been completed, then repeat Rows 1–58 as necessary, ending when you have about 2" (5 cm) of band left to embroider. Check the length of the band against the front opening again. If the band has tightened up and become too short to fit around the front opening, return the live sts to larger needle, work another 29 rows for band, check the fit again, and return sts to holder once more. Embroider the rem rows in patt. Carefully remove waste yarn from base of provisional CO and place sts at each end of band on a separate dpn. With MC threaded on a tapestry needle and using the Kitchener st, graft live sts to sts from base of CO. If your motif colors do not happen to match on either side of the join, position the join at the center of the lower back where it will be inconspicuous.

Finishing

With MC threaded on a tapestry needle, sew sleeve seams. Fold cuff facings to WS along fold lines and sew invisibly in place. Fold band in half along fold line. Beg with grafted seam of band at center of lower back, pin band evenly all the way around the front opening so that embroidered half of band corresponds to RS of garment, easing in any fullness. With MC threaded on a tapestry needle, use a backstitch to sew selvedge of embroidered half of band to body. Fold band to WS along fold line, and sew facing invisibly in place along other selvedge. With MC threaded on a tapestry needle, backstitch through both layers of band just outside the outermost dark brown embroidery line to secure the fold.

Wash in cold water with mild soap or shampoo and rinse with hair conditioner. Lay flat to dry. When slightly damp, lightly steam-block sleeves and back on WS.

Short Cape

A tapestry recovered from the Incan Pachaca-amac—a cloister for women who devoted their lives to creating textiles—featuring one the most ubiquitous pre-Columbian motifs became the basis for this cape. The cape is worked from the bottom up in eight panels separated by columns of twisted stitches and decorated with bold stripes and intarsia color patterns. The front is fastened with three ceramic buttons. Position the closure at the center front or skewed to one side, depending on where you want the color pattern on the back to fall.

Finished Size 131" (332.5 cm) circumference at lower edge, including width of 2" (5 cm) right front button band; 15" (38 cm) circumference at neck, buttoned; and 23" (58.5 cm) long from base of collar to finished lower edge.

Yarn CYCA #3 Light (DK weight). *Shown here:* The Alpaca Yarn Company Classic Alpaca (100% superfine alpaca, 110 yd [100 m]/50 g): #1400 prairie green, 8 skeins; #1800 Ozark purple, 7 skeins; #2212 hazelnut (brown), #2406 butternut (gold), and #2201 sweet potato (orange), 2 skeins each.

Needles Size 7 (4.5 mm) and 6 (4 mm): 40" (100 cm) circular (cir). Adjust needle size if necessary to obtain the correct gauge.

Notions A few yards (meters) of waste yarn and smooth satin ribbon for provisional cast-on; markers (m); stitch holders; tapestry needle; three 1¼" (3.2 cm) buttons; sewing needle and thread for attaching buttons.

Gauge 20½ sts and 26 rows = 4" (10 cm) in St st using larger needle; 4 sts of right twist patt measure about ⅝" (1.5 cm) wide, relaxed, using larger needle.

Stitch Guide

Right Twist (worked over 4 sts)
All RS Rows: P1, knit into front of second st on left-hand needle but leave st on the needle, knit the first st on left-hand needle, then slip both sts off needle tog, p1.
All WS Rows: K1, p2, k1.

Note: When working right twists in lower border from charts, work each right twist st in same color as sts on either side. Work right twist patt at center back in purple throughout.

Notes

• Cape is worked in one piece from the lower edge to the collar.

• Work all charts using the intarsia method (see Glossary, page 135), twisting yarns on WS at color changes to prevent holes. You may find it more convenient to use 2- to 3-yard (2- to 3-meter) pieces for each color section, joining new strands as needed, rather than working from small yarn balls or butterflies.

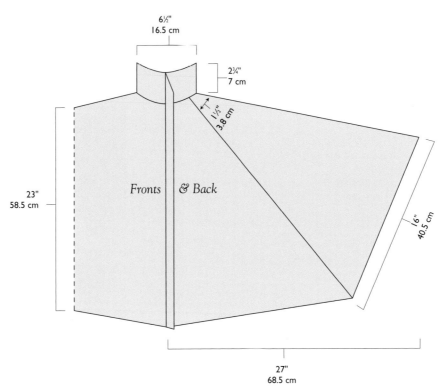

6½"
16.5 cm

2¾"
7 cm

1½"
3.8 cm

23"
58.5 cm

Fronts & *Back*

16"
40.5 cm

27"
68.5 cm

Cape

With larger needle, waste yarn and ribbon, and using the ribbon method provisional cast-on (see Glossary, page 131), CO 668 sts. Change to purple and work 1 RS row, placing markers (pm) as foll: K80 for right front, pm, *work 4 sts in right twist patt (see Stitch Guide), pm, k80; rep from * 5 more times, work 4 sts in right twist patt, pm, k80 for left front—eight 80-st sections; seven 4-st sections in right twist patt. Cont working right twist patt on marked 4-st sections and rem sts in St st for 1 WS row. *Dec row:* (RS) K2, k2tog, *knit to 2 sts before m, ssk, slip marker (sl m), work 4 sts in right twist, sl m, k2tog; rep from * 6 more times, knit to last 4 sts, ssk, k2—16 sts dec'd. Work 3 rows even. Rep the last 4 rows 3 more times, then work 1 more dec row, then work 1 more WS row even—588 sts rem; eight 70-st sections; seven 4-st right twist sections; 20 rows

completed with purple; piece measures about 3" (7.5 cm) from CO, measured straight up along a single column of sts; do not measure along diagonal shaping lines. Set up patts from Row 1 of charts (see page 110) as foll (see Notes): (RS) Work Chart 1 over 70 sts for right front, sl m, work 4 sts right twist, sl m, work Chart 2 over 70 sts for right side front, sl m, work 4 sts right twist, sl m, work Chart 1 over 70 sts for right side back, sl m, work 4 sts right twist, sl m, work Right Back chart (see page 111) over 70 sts, sl m, work 4 sts right twist, sl m, work Left Back chart over 70 sts, sl m, work 4 sts right twist, sl m, work Chart 2 over 70 sts for left side back, sl m, work 4 sts right twist, sl m, work Chart 1 over 70 sts for left side front, sl m, work 4 sts right twist, sl m, work Chart 2 over 70 sts for left front. Working dec row as before on Rows 3, 7, and 11 of charts, work in patt until Row 12 of charts has

been completed—540 sts rem; eight 64-st sections; seven 4-st right twist sections. Using orange for fronts and all 4 side sections, and cont back sections as charted and right twists as established, work in St st for 22 rows, and *at the same time* work dec row 5 more times corresponding to Rows 15, 19, 23, 27, and 31 of back charts—460 sts rem; eight 54-st sections; seven 4-st right twist sections. Work in patts until Row 34 of back charts has been completed. Using green for fronts and all 4 side sections, and cont back sections as charted and right twists as established, work 1 RS dec row (Row 35 of back charts)—444 sts rem; eight 52-st sections; seven 4-st right twist sections. On the next WS row (Row 36 of back charts), cont back charts and right twist sections in patt, and knit all green sts on WS for garter ridge. Cont back sections as charted and right twist as established, work rem sts in St st with green, working dec row every 4th row until Row 130 of back charts has been completed—76 sts rem; eight 6-st sections; seven 4-st right twist sections; piece measures about 23" (58.5 cm) from CO measured straight up along a single column of sts. Place sts on holder.

Lower Edge Hem

Carefully remove waste yarn from base of provisional CO and place 668 sts of lower edge on smaller needle. Join purple with WS facing and knit 1 WS row for fold line, placing markers as foll: *K80, pm, k4, pm; rep from * 7 more times, k80—eight 80-st sections; seven 4-st sections. Work 2 rows even in St st, ending with a WS row. *Dec row:* (RS) K2, k2tog, *knit to 2 sts before m, ssk, slip marker (sl m), k4, sl m, k2tog; rep from * 6 more times, knit to last 4 sts, ssk, k2—16 sts dec'd. Work 3 rows even. Rep the last 4 rows 3 more times, then work 1 more dec row, then work 1 more WS row even—588 sts rem; eight 70-st sections; seven 4-st sections; 20 rows completed with purple from fold line. Fold hem to WS along fold line, and with purple threaded on a tapestry needle, graft live sts of hem to main body (see Glossary, page 134) along the top row of purple on RS of cape.

Left Front Facing

With RS facing, smaller needle, and beg at top of left front, pick up and knit 112 sts (about 3 sts

for every 4 rows) along selvedge of left front, using colors to match patt on left front. Working facing in St st intarsia, knit 1 WS row for fold line. Work even in St st using established colors for 12 rows, ending with a WS row. Loosely BO all sts. Fold facing to WS along fold line and with matching colors threaded on a tapestry needle, use a backstitch (see Glossary, page 136) to sew facing in place. Sew selvedge of facing invisibly to top edge of hem.

Right Front Buttonhole Band

With RS facing, purple, larger needle, and beg at lower right front edge, pick up and knit 112 sts (about 3 sts for every 4 rows) along selvedge of right front. Knit 1 WS row for garter ridge. Work 4 rows even in St st, ending with a WS row. *Buttonhole row:* (RS) Knit to last 38 sts, *BO 3 sts, k16; rep from * once more. *Next row:* (WS) *Purl to gap made by buttonhole, use the cable method (see Glossary, page 131) to CO 3 sts over the gap to complete buttonhole; rep from * once more, purl to end. Work 6 more rows even in St st, ending with a WS row—12 rows completed from garter ridge. Purl 1 RS row for fold line. Change to smaller needle and work in St st for 7 rows, ending with a WS row. Rep buttonhole row, then CO over gaps on foll WS row to complete buttonholes as before. Work 4 rows even in St st. Fold band

in half along fold line and with purple threaded on a tapestry needle, graft live sts of band to main body, sewing along the "ditch" of the pick-up row (see Glossary, page 134). Sew selvedge of hem invisibly to edge of band on WS. With purple threaded on a tapestry needle, work buttonhole stitch (see Glossary, page 133), around buttonholes to join both layers.

Collar

With purple, larger needle, and RS facing, pick up and knit 10 sts along top edge of buttonhole band, picking up through both layers of band. Place 76 held neck sts on left-hand end of needle and knit to end—86 sts total. Knit 1 WS row for garter ridge. Shape ends of collar using short-rows

Chart 1

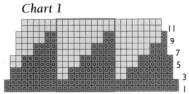

11
9
7
5
3
1

Chart 2

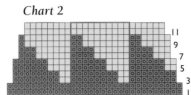

11
9
7
5
3
1

■ green; k on RS, p on WS

□ green; k on WS

gold

+ orange

○ brown

◆ purple

□ pattern repeat

Left Back

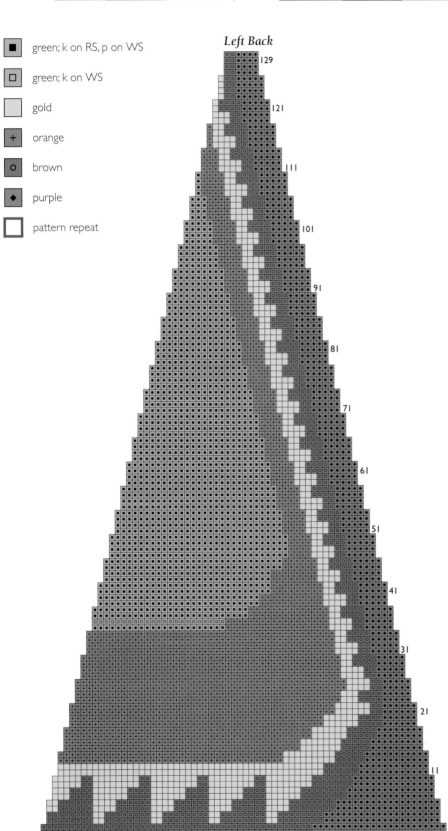

129

121

111

101

91

81

71

61

51

41

31

21

11

1

(see Glossary, page 136) and work buttonhole as foll:

Row 1: (RS) Knit to last st, wrap last st, turn.

Row 2: Purl to last st, wrap last st, turn.

Row 3: K4, BO 3 sts for buttonhole, knit to 1 st before previously wrapped st, wrap next st, turn.

Row 4: Purl to buttonhole gap, use the cable method to CO 3 sts, purl to 1 st before previously wrapped st, wrap next st, turn.

Row 5: Knit to 1 st before previously wrapped st, wrap next st, turn.

Row 6: Purl to 1 st before previously wrapped st, wrap next st, turn.

Rows 7–18: Rep Rows 5 and 6 six more times—after completing Row 18 there will be 9 wrapped sts at each end of row; collar measures about 2¾" (7 cm) from pick-up row at highest point.

Change to smaller needle, and reverse short-row shaping as foll:

Row 19: (RS) Purl for fold line to wrapped st, work wrapped st tog with its wrap, wrap next st, turn (2 wraps on last st).

Row 20: Purl to wrapped st, work wrapped st tog with its wrap, wrap next st, turn (2 wraps on last st).

Row 21: Knit to double-wrapped st, work st tog with both wraps, wrap next st, turn.

Row 22: Purl to double-wrapped

st, work st tog with both wraps, wrap next st, turn.

Rows 23–32: Rep Rows 21 and 22 five times.

Row 33: K4, BO 3 sts for buttonhole, knit to double-wrapped st, work st tog with both wraps, wrap next st, turn.

Row 34: Purl to buttonhole gap, use the cable method to CO 3 sts, purl to double-wrapped st, work st tog with both wraps, wrap next st, turn.

Row 35: Knit to end, working rem wrapped st tog with its wraps.

Row 36: Purl to end, working rem wrapped st tog with its wraps.

Fold collar along fold line and with purple threaded on a tapestry needle, use the backstitch grafting method to secure live sts of collar to base of collar, sewing along the "ditch" of the pick-up row. With purple threaded on a tapestry needle, work buttonhole stitch around collar buttonhole to join both layers.

Finishing

Weave in loose ends. With sewing needle and thread, sew buttons to left front opposite buttonholes. Wash in cold water with mild soap or shampoo and rinse with hair conditioner. Lay flat to dry. When slightly damp, block lightly on WS with a steam iron.

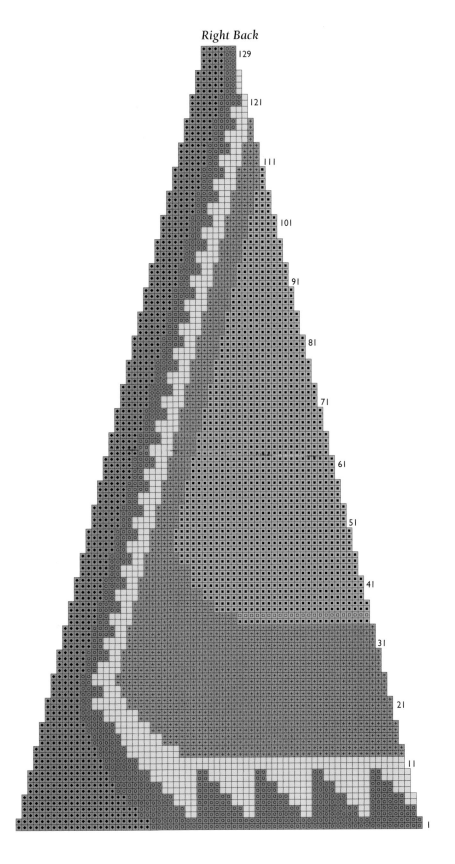

Right Back

Geometric Scarf

Originally, I designed this scarf as a knitting project for a guided tour of Peru. I wanted to give the participants an opportunity to translate a simple but beautiful tapestry pattern into a warm and comfortable scarf. In my interpretation, I've enlarged the dimensions of the traditional geometric stepped pattern to accommodate stitches knitted with worsted-weight alpaca. The blocks of color are worked in the intarsia style of knitting in rich earth tones. All four edges are finished with a narrow band of black stockinette stitch.

Finished Size About 8" (20.5 cm) wide and 100" (254 cm) long.
Yarn CYCA #3 Light (DK weight). *Shown here:* The Alpaca Yarn Company Classic Alpaca (100% superfine alpaca; 110 yd [100 m]/50 g): #0500 black, 3 skeins; #2406 butternut (gold), #2000 California claret (red), #2213 cayenne (orange-red), #2023 flame (medium brown), and #2211 mahogany (dark brown), 1 skein each. *Note:* The optional black edging uses 2 skeins of yarn; if omitting the edging, you will only need 1 skein of black.

Needles Size 6 (4 mm): straight. Adjust needle size if necessary to obtain the correct gauge.
Notions Tapestry needle.
Gauge 20 sts and 23½ rows = 4" (10 cm) in double seed st.

Stitch Guide
Double Seed Stitch:
(multiple of 4 sts)
Rows 1 and 2: *K2, p2; rep from *.
Rows 3 and 4: *P2, k2; rep from *.
Repeat Rows 1–4 for pattern.

Note
This scarf is not truly reversible. On the right side, there will be small "blips" of color when a stitch worked in the previous color is purled with a new color. These blips will appear on the wrong side as well, but the wrong side will also have a vertical running stitch effect where the yarns are twisted at the color changes. If you twist the yarns consistently for a tidy effect, each face of the scarf will have a slightly different but equally attractive appearance.

Scarf

CO 20 sts with black, then CO 20 more sts with gold—40 sts total; when piece is turned to beg the first row, the gold sts will be worked first. Work in double seed st (see Stitch Guide) as foll, twisting yarns on the WS at color changes, instarsia style (see Glossary, page 135), to prevent forming holes.

Row 1: (RS) Work 20 sts gold, 20 sts black.

Rows 2–12: Work even in established colors.

Row 13: Work 10 sts dark brown, 20 sts gold, 10 sts black.

Rows 14–24: Work even in established colors.

Row 25: Work 20 sts dark brown, 20 sts gold.

Rows 26–36: Work even in established colors.

Row 37: Work 10 sts medium brown, 20 sts dark brown, 10 sts gold.

Rows 38–48: Work even in established colors.

Row 49: Work 20 sts medium brown, 20 sts dark brown.

Rows 50–60: Work even in established colors.

Row 61: Work 10 sts orange-red, 20 sts medium brown, 10 sts dark brown.

Rows 62–72: Work even in established colors.

Row 73: Work 20 sts orange-red, 20 sts medium brown.

Rows 74–84: Work even in established colors.

Row 85: Work 10 sts red, 20 sts orange-red, 10 sts medium brown.

Rows 86–96: Work even in established colors.

Row 97: Work 20 sts red, 20 sts orange-red.

Rows 98–108: Work even in established colors.

Row 109: Work 10 sts black, 20 sts red, 10 sts orange-red.

Rows 110–120: Work even in established colors.

Row 121: Work 20 sts black, 20 sts red.

Rows 122–132: Work even in established colors.

Row 133: Work 10 sts gold, 20 sts black, 10 sts red.

Rows 134–144: Work even in established colors.

Rep Rows 1–144 three more times, then work Rows 1–12 once more to end with a block of 20 gold sts and 20 black sts to match the color blocks at beg of scarf—588 patt rows completed; piece should measure about 100" (254 cm) from CO. Loosely BO all sts in patt with their corresponding colors.

Finishing

Weave in all loose ends.

Edging

(optional) With black, CO 6 sts. Work even in St st until piece measures 216" (548.5 cm) from CO. Place sts temporarily on a piece of waste yarn, and do not BO. With black threaded on a tapestry needle and RS facing, use a backstitch (see Glossary, page 136) to sew edging around all four sides of scarf, leaving the last 2" (5 cm) free for adjustment later. Fold edging around edge of scarf and use a slip stitch (see Glossary, page 136) to sew it in place, with the edging covering the backstitches and making sure that the slip stitches don't show on the other side of the scarf. Add or remove rows at the end of the edging if necessary to obtain a perfect fit, then sew the live sts to the CO sts as invisibly as possible. Sew the rem 2" (5 cm) of edging to scarf.

Wash in cold water with mild soap or shampoo and rinse with hair conditioner. Lay flat to dry. When slightly damp, lightly steam-block on WS.

Breeding Alpacas Today

I love alpacas! I love their cute faces, gentle disposition, and soft humming. I love their fleeces of whisper-light fiber that spins into luxurious yarn. On a practical note, alpacas are ideal livestock. They are efficient foragers—five animals can subsist on a single acre of land. They are resistant to disease, so vet bills are minimal. They are clean, confining their waste to specific areas. And they are environmentally friendly—the soft pads of their feet don't tear up pastures. Because their primary market value is in their fiber, alpacas don't have to be killed for profit; the same animal provides profit year after year. Because females produce offspring only once a year, it takes decades for herds to grow, which ensures their value. Since approval of export from South America in the early 1980s, the alpaca industry has grown steadily in the United States and other countries, but even so, it lags far behind that of South America.

Although I now raise alpacas myself, I didn't even know what an alpaca looked like until 1999 when I read a magazine advertisement that expounded upon the merits of raising alpacas as a source of income and a fulfilling lifestyle. I discovered that you don't need a college degree or background in farming to succeed in raising alpacas. Thanks to their easygoing nature and self-sufficiency, even children can successfully care for the animals. And the virtues of alpaca fiber are many. Alpaca fiber is oil-free and hollow, which means that it has little dander and is soft to the touch, while at the same time superbly insulating. It comes in a wide range of natural colors—twenty-two in all—so the product you buy is likely to be completely natural, chemical-free, and nonallergenic. Moreover, the fiber is soil-resistant, so it only takes a little clean water to rinse away most dirt.

Photo courtesy of Carol Ropp

Every spring, alpacas are sheared to harvest their precious fiber crop. Each animal produces about five pounds of usable fiber. The fleeces are hand-picked of vegetable matter and debris, then gently cleaned with soapy water. The cleaned fiber is separated into bundles according to the fineness of the fiber before being sent for processing. Coarse fibers are used for rugs, blankets, and socks; fine fibers are used for sweaters, mittens, hats, and scarves; the finest fibers, which are comparable to cashmere, are used for luxurious clothing that is worn next to the skin. Many alpaca owners spin their own fiber, while others send it to a commercial mill for processing. Still others send it to a cooperative of alpaca farmers who pool their fiber for processing into yarns, fabrics, and finished apparel. Each step in processing the fiber yields greater return for the farmer, so many alpaca farms sell everything from fleece to yarn to finished garments and accessories directly to the public. Other farmers sell their products at fairs, markets, and specialty shops. Even if there isn't an alpaca farm near where you live, thanks to the Internet, these luxurious products are only a few clicks away. Alpaca, once the fabric of Incan kings, is now available to everyone.

Yes, I love alpacas!

—Carol A. Ropp
Tanasi Trace Alpacas

Bolero

Inspired by the traditional short jacket worn by highland women even today, this bolero combines border details from two different Chancay tapestries. The back and fronts are worked in four geometric color-work panels with similar color-work motifs repeated at the cuffs. Mitered corners shape the color-work panels with crisp edges, and the neck, fronts, lower hem, and cuffs are finished with tucks.

Finished Size 37 (40, 46)" (94 [101.5, 117] cm) bust circumference. *Note:* Front edges of bolero deliberately do not meet at center front, and therefore the garment can accommodate a slightly smaller or larger bust size.

Yarn CYCA #3 Light (DK weight). *Shown here:* The Alpaca Yarn Company Classic Alpaca (100% superfine alpaca; 110 yd [100 m]/50 g): #0500 black (MC), 9 (10, 11) skeins; #2406 butternut (gold), #2201 sweet potato (orange), #2213 cayenne (orange-red), and #2000 California claret (red), 4 skeins each.

Needles Size 7 (4.5 mm): straight, and 32" (80 cm) circular (cir). Size 6 (4 mm): straight, and 32" (80 cm) cir. Adjust needle size if necessary to obtain the correct gauge.

Notions A few yards (meters) of waste yarn and smooth satin ribbon for provisional cast-on; markers (m); stitch holders; tapestry needle.

Gauge 19½ sts and 25 rows = 4" (10 cm) in St st color work from charts using larger needles; 18½ sts and 29 rows = 4" (10 cm) in solid-color St st using smaller needles for center back panel; 18 sts and 25 rows = 4" (10 cm) in solid-color St st using larger needles for sleeves.

Stitch Guide

Mitered Decreases: On RS rows, knit to 2 sts before marker, ssk (see Glossary, page 133), slip marker (sl m), k1, sl m, k2tog. On WS rows, purl to 2 sts before marker, p2tog, sl m, p1, sl m, ssp (see Glossary, page 133). *Note:* Work decreases using the color of the patt sts on either side of marked st. Decrease symbols are not shown on chart.

Left Back

With larger straight needles, waste yarn and ribbon, and using the ribbon method provisional cast-on (see Glossary, page 131), CO 125 (129, 131) sts. Change to gold and knit 1 RS row (counts as Row 1 of Left Back chart), placing markers (pm) as foll: K83, pm, k1, pm, k41 (45, 47). Beg with Row 2, cont in patt from Left Back chart (see page 121) according to your size, and working mitered decreases (see Stitch Guide) on every row except Rows 5, 19, and 33 (MC garter ridge rows), until Row 39 of chart has been completed—55 (59, 61) sts rem; 48 sts before first m at beg of RS row, 1 st between markers, 6 (10, 12) sts at end of row after second m; piece measures about 6¼" (16 cm) from CO, measured straight up along a single column of sts (do not measure along diagonal miter line). Place sts on holder or waste yarn.

Right Back

With larger straight needles, waste yarn and ribbon, and using the ribbon method provisional cast-on, CO 125 (129, 131) sts. Change to gold and knit 1 RS row (counts as Row 1 of Right Back chart), placing markers (pm) as foll: K41 (45, 47), pm, k1, pm, k83. Beg with Row 2, cont in patt from Right Back chart according to your size, and working mitered decreases on every row except Rows 5, 19, and 33 (MC garter ridge rows). Cont in this manner until Row 39 of chart has been completed—55 (59, 61) sts rem; 6 (10, 12) sts at beg of RS row before first m, 1 st between markers, 48 sts at end of row after second m; piece measures about 6¼" (16 cm) from CO measured straight up along a single column of sts (do not measure along diagonal miter line). Place sts on holder or waste yarn.

Back Tucks

Carefully remove waste yarn from provisional CO of left back to expose 84 sts (83 sts from long edge plus 1 mitered corner st) and place sts on larger straight needle; leave waste yarn and ribbon at base of rem 41 (45, 47) sts. Join MC with RS facing, and work in St st for 6 rows, ending with a WS row. *Tuck row:* (RS) Fold the 6 rows of St st just worked in half with wrong sides touching to bring the sts on needle next to first row of sts. *Insert tip of right-hand needle into the first st on left-hand needle and then into the loop of the MC purl "bump" 6 rows below, lift the purl loop onto the left-hand needle, k2tog (st on needle tog with lifted loop), slip original st from left-hand needle; rep from * across, making sure that each k2tog joins sts that line up vertically one above the other from the same st column—still

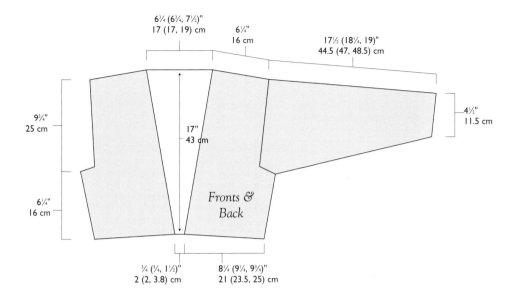

6¾ (6¾, 7½)"
17 (17, 19) cm

6¼"
16 cm

17½ (18¼, 19)"
44.5 (47, 48.5) cm

9¾"
25 cm

17"
43 cm

4½"
11.5 cm

6¼"
16 cm

*Fronts &
Back*

¾ (¾, 1½)"
2 (2, 3.8) cm

8¼ (9¼, 9¾)"
21 (23.5, 25) cm

84 sts. Place sts on holder or waste yarn. Rep for right back, and leave sts on needle; the mitered corner st should be closest to the needle tip.

Center Back Panel

Return 84 sts of left back to larger straight needle with RS facing and mitered corner st closest to the needle tip. With MC and smaller straight needles, use the cable method (see Glossary, page 131) to CO 3 (3, 7) sts. Work center back panel in St st, joining to left and right backs at end of each row as foll:

Row 1: (RS) Knit to last st of center back, sl last st to right-hand needle as if to knit with yarn in back (kwise wyb), k1 from left back, pass slipped st over (psso)—1 st joined from left back.

Row 2: Purl to last st of center back, sl last st to right-hand needle as if to knit with yarn in front (kwise wyf), p1 from right back, psso—1 st joined from right back.

Row 3: Knit to last st of center back, sl last st to right-hand needle kwise wyb, k1 from left back, psso, knit 1 more st from left back—2 sts joined from left back; 1 st added to center back panel.

Row 4: Purl to last st of center back, sl last st to right-hand needle kwise wyf, p1 from right back, psso, purl 1 more st from right back—2 sts joined from right back; 1 st added to center back panel.

Rows 5–10: Rep Rows 1 and 2 three times.

Rows 11 and 12: Rep Rows 3 and 4 once.

Rows 13–18: Rep Rows 1 and 2 three times.

Rows 19 and 20: Rep Rows 3 and 4 once.

Rows 21–40: Rep Rows 1–20 once more. When Row 40 has been completed there will be 15 (15, 19) center back panel sts; 26 sts each joined from left and right backs; 58 sts rem for each back.

Rows 41 and 42: Rep Rows 1 and 2 once.

Rows 43 and 44: Rep Rows 3 and 4 once—17 (17, 21) center back panel sts; 55 sts each rem for right and left backs.

Rows 45 and 46: Rep Rows 1 and 2 once.

Row 47: Knit to last st of center back, sl last st to right-hand needle kwise wyb, k2tog from left back, psso—2 sts joined from left back *without* adding a st to center back panel.

Row 48: Purl to last st of center back, sl last st to right-hand needle kwise wyf, p2tog from right back, psso—2 sts joined from right back *without* adding a st to center back panel.

Rows 49–56: Rep Rows 41–48 once.

Rows 57–60: Rep Rows 1 and 2 two times. When Row 60 has been completed there will be 19 (19, 23) center back panel sts; 44 sts rem for each back.

Rows 61–100: Rep Rows 41–60 two more times. When Row 100 has been completed there will be 27 (27, 31) center back panel sts; 16 sts rem for each back.

Rows 101 and 102: Rep Rows 3 and 4 once.

Rows 103–106: Rep Rows 1 and 2 two times.

Rows 107 and 108: Rep Rows 47 and 48 once.

Rows 109–112: Rep Rows 1 and 2 two times.

Rows 113–124: Rep Rows 101–112 once—31 (31, 35) center back panel sts; all sts have been joined from left and

right backs; center back panel measures 17" (43 cm) from CO, measured straight up the middle (do not measure along shaped sides of panel). Place center back panel sts on holder or waste yarn.

Right Front
Work as for left back.

Left Front
Work as for right back.

Shoulder Tucks
With MC, larger straight needles, and RS facing, pick up and knit 29 sts along shoulder selvedge of left back (about 3 sts for every 4 rows). Work in St st for 6 rows, ending with a RS row. BO all sts. Rep for right back shoulder. Fold each tuck in half with wrong sides of fabric touching, and with MC threaded on a tapestry needle sew BO edge to CO edge of each tuck. With MC, sew back and fronts tog along shoulder selvedges, leaving tucks free to show on RS.

Left Armhole Tuck
Place 55 (59, 61) held sts from armhole edge of left back on larger straight or cir needle with RS facing, then place 55 (59, 61) sts held sts from armhole edge of left front on same needle—110 (118, 122). Join MC with RS facing; sts to be worked first should be the left front sts; row begins at base of armhole. Next row: (RS) *[K2tog, k2] 2 times, k2tog, k1; rep from

* to last 0 (8, 12) sts; for size 40" end [k2tog, k2] 2 times; for size 46" end [k4, k2tog] 2 times—80 (86, 90) sts rem. Work 1 WS row even in St st. Cont in St st, working short-rows shaping (see Glossary, page 136) as foll:

Row 1: (RS) Knit to last 16 sts, wrap next st, turn.

Row 2: Purl to last 16 sts, wrap next st, turn.

Row 3: Knit to 10 sts before previously wrapped st, wrap next st, turn.

Row 4: Purl to 10 sts before previously wrapped st, wrap next st, turn.

Rows 5 and 6: Rep Rows 3 and 4 once more—outermost wrapped sts are the 36th sts from each end of the row; 8 (14, 18) sts at center between innermost wrapped sts.

Row 7: Knit to first wrapped st, work wrapped st tog with its wrap, knit to foll wrapped st, work wrapped st tog with its wrap, wrap next st, turn.

Row 8: Purl to first wrapped st, work wrapped st tog with its wrap, purl to foll wrapped st, work wrapped st tog with its wrap, wrap next st, turn.

Rows 9 and 10: Rep Rows 7 and 8.

Rows 11 and 12: Work to end in St st, working rem wrapped sts tog with their wraps as you come to them.

Work 2 rows even in St st—tuck is 16 rows high at shoulder line in center, and 6 rows high at each

Left Sleeve

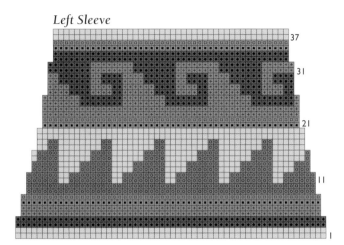

Right Sleeve

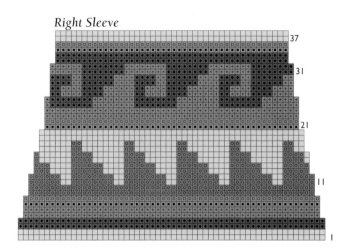

Right Back

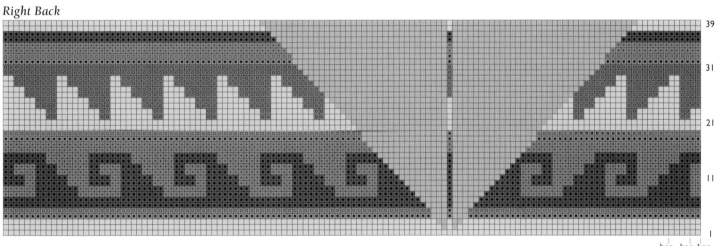

beg beg beg
37"   40"   46"

Left Back

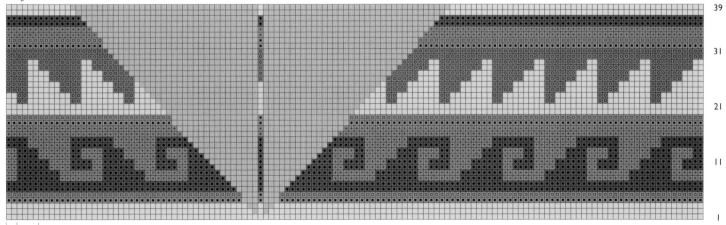

end end end
46" 40" 37"

Left Sleeve

Place a removable marker or safety pin in the center of the sts on the needle—40 (43, 45) sts on each side of marker.

Shape Sleeve Cap

Cont working in St st on 80 (86, 90) armhole sts from tuck, using short-rows to shape sleeve cap as foll:

Row 1: (RS) Knit to 8 sts beyond center m, wrap next st, turn.

Row 2: Purl to 8 sts beyond center m, wrap next st, turn.

Row 3: Knit to previously wrapped st, work wrapped st tog with its wrap, k8, wrap next st, turn.

Row 4: Purl to previously wrapped st, work wrapped st tog with its wrap, p8, wrap next st, turn.

Row 5: Knit to previously wrapped st, work wrapped st tog with its wrap, k4, wrap next st, turn.

Row 6: Purl to previously wrapped st, work wrapped st tog with its wrap, p4, wrap next st, turn.

Rows 7–10: Rep Rows 5 and 6 two times.

Row 11: Knit to previously wrapped st, work wrapped st tog with its wrap, k2, wrap next st, turn.

Row 12: Purl to previously wrapped st, work wrapped st tog with its wrap, p2, wrap next st, turn.

Rows 13–20: Rep Rows 11 and 12 four times.

Work 2 rows in St st across all sts, working rem wrapped sts tog with their wraps as you come to them—still 80 (86, 90) sts; sleeve

measures about 3½" (9 cm) from beg of cap, measured straight up at center.

Shape Sleeve

Dec row: (RS) K2, ssk, knit to last 4 sts, k2tog, k2—2 sts dec'd. Work 3 (1, 1) row(s) even. Rep the shaping of the last 4 (2, 2) rows 9 (1, 3) more time(s)—60 (82, 82) sts rem. Rep dec row, then work 5 (3, 3) rows even—58 (80, 80) sts. Rep the shaping of the last 0 (4, 4) rows 0 (11, 11) more times—58 sts rem for all sizes; sleeve measures about 11 (11¾, 12½)" (28 [30, 31.5] cm) from beg of cap, measured straight up the center. Work Rows 1–38 of Left Sleeve chart, dec 1 st at each end of row every 4 rows 5 times, then every 6 rows 2 times—44 sts rem when Row 38 has been completed. With MC, work 6 rows even in St st.

Tuck row: (RS) Fold last 6 rows in half with wrong sides touching to bring the sts on needle next to first MC row. *Insert tip of right-hand needle into the first st on left-hand needle and then into the loop of the MC purl "bump" at the base of the same st column, lift the purl loop onto the left-hand needle, k2tog (st on needle tog with lifted loop), slip original st from left-hand needle; rep from * across, making sure that each k2tog joins sts that line up vertically one above the other from the same st column—still 44 sts; sleeve measures about 17½ (18¼, 19)" (44.5 [46.5, 48.5] cm) from beg of cap.

selvedge. *Tuck row:* (RS) Fold tuck in half with wrong sides touching to bring the sts on needle next to first row of picked-up sts. *Insert tip of right-hand needle into the first st on left-hand needle and then into the loop of the MC purl "bump" at the base of the same st column, lift the purl loop onto the left-hand needle, k2tog (st on needle tog with lifted loop), slip original st from left-hand needle; rep from * across, making sure that each k2tog joins sts that line up vertically one above the other from the same st column—still 80 (86, 90) sts. Purl 1 WS row.

Cuff Facing

Change to smaller straight needles. Work even in St st with MC for 16 rows, inc 1 st at each end of needle on 3rd, 7th, 11th, and 15th rows—52 sts. Loosely BO all sts.

Right Armhole Tuck

Work as for left armhole tuck.

Right Sleeve

Work as for left sleeve until 58 sts rem for all sizes—sleeve measures about 11 (11¾, 12½)" (28 [30, 31.5] cm) from beg of cap, measured straight up the center. Complete as for left sleeve, but substitute Right Sleeve chart for Left Sleeve chart.

Side Tucks

With MC, larger straight needles, and RS facing, pick up and knit 29 sts along side selvedge of right front (about 3 sts for every 4 rows). Work in St st for 6 rows, ending with a RS row. BO all sts. Rep for side selvedge of left front. Fold each tuck in half with wrong sides of fabric touching, and with MC threaded on a tapestry needle, sew BO edge to CO edge of each tuck. With MC, sew back and fronts tog along side selvedges, leaving tucks free to show on RS.

Body Facing

Carefully remove waste yarn from provisional CO of right front to expose 125 (129, 131) sts and place sts on larger cir needle. Join

MC with RS facing. K41 (45, 47) sts of lower right front, pm, k1 corner st, pm, k83 along right front opening, pm, return 31 (31, 35) held sts of center back panel to needle and knit across them, pm. Carefully remove waste yarn from provisional CO of left front to expose 125 (129, 131) sts and transfer sts to cir needle with RS facing. K83 sts along left front opening, pm, k1 corner st, pm, k41 (45, 47) sts of lower left front. Carefully remove waste yarn from provisional CO of lower left back to expose 41 (45, 47) sts and transfer sts to cir needle with RS facing. K41 (45, 47) sts of left back, pick up and knit 3 (3, 7) sts across lower edge of center back panel. Carefully remove waste yarn from provisional CO of lower right back to expose 41 (45, 47) sts and transfer sts to cir needle with RS facing. K41 (45, 47) sts of right back to finish where you began at right side seam—366 (382, 398) sts total. Join for working in the rnd and pm to indicate beg of rnd. Knit 5 more rnds—6 rnds total completed. *Tuck rnd:* Fold last 6 rnds in half with wrong sides touching to bring the sts on needle next to MC pick-up row. *Insert tip of right-hand needle into the first st on left-hand needle and then into the loop of the MC purl "bump" at the base of the same st column, lift the purl loop onto the left-hand needle, k2tog (st on needle

tog with lifted loop), slip original st from left-hand needle; rep from * to end, making sure that each k2tog joins sts that line up vertically one above the other from the same st column—still 366 (382, 398) sts. Change to smaller cir needle.

Shape Facing Corners

Knit to 2 sts before lower right front corner m, *ssk, sl m, k1, sl m, k2tog,* knit to right shoulder m, sl m, k1f&b, knit to 1 st before left shoulder m, k1f&b, sl m, knit to 2 sts before lower left front corner m, rep from * to * once more, knit to end of rnd—2 sts dec'd at each lower corner; 1 st inc'd on each side of back neck. Rep the last rnd 15 more times—334 (350, 366) sts rem; 16 rnds completed from tuck rnd. Loosely BO all sts.

Finishing

Weave in loose ends. Secure body facing using MC threaded on a tapestry needle, backstitching (see Glossary, page 136) precisely along MC garter st stripe on RS, except for around the back of the neck where you should secure facing as invisibly as possible so black stitching yarn doesn't show on RS. Secure cuff facings in the same manner. Sew sleeve seams. Wash in cold water with mild soap or shampoo and rinse with hair conditioner. Lay flat to dry. When slightly damp, lightly steam-block on WS.

Bohemian Poncho and Beret

Ponchos have been worn in the Andean highlands since time immemorial. This trendy garment was readily adopted by other cultures and is now worn by soldiers, sportsmen, and fashionable women alike. Being naturally water repellent, alpaca is particularly appropriate for outerwear. My interpretation of the ageless poncho is worked from the turtleneck downward in wide bias strips shaped with short-rows to flare at the lower edge. The strips alternate between stockinette stitch and reverse stockinette stitch and the boundaries between them are embellished with stem stitch embroidery. The coordinating beret is shaped with short-rows.

Finished Size Poncho: 46" (117 cm) circumference measured about 6" (15 cm) down from base of turtle neck, 90" (229 cm) circumference at lower edge, and about 24" (61 cm) long from base of turtleneck to lower edge. Beret: 22" (56 cm) circumference with rib brim relaxed, will stretch to 23" (58.5 cm).

Yarn CYCA #4 Medium (worsted weight). *Shown here:* The Fibre Company Fauna Zorro (70% baby alpaca, 30% merino wool; 80 yd [73 m]/ 50 g): black, 2 skeins for poncho; 1 skein for beret.

CYCA #4 Medium (worsted weight). *Shown here:* The Fibre Company Fauna Starry Night (50% alpaca, 20% kid mohair, 20% wool, 10% Soy Silk; 70 yd [64 m]/50 g): charcoal heather, 15 skeins for poncho; 2 skeins for beret.

CYCA #3 Light (DK weight). *Shown here:* The Alpaca Yarn Company Classic Alpaca (100% superfine alpaca, 110 yd [100 m]/50 g): #2055 patriot red, 1 skein each for poncho and beret.

Needles Size 9 (5.5 mm): 16" (40 cm) and 24" (60 cm) circular (cir) and set of 4 or 5 double-pointed (dpn); spare 24" (60 cm) cir and dpn same size or smaller than main needle. Adjust needle size if necessary to obtain the correct gauge.

Notions Markers (m); stitch holders or contrasting waste yarn; tapestry needle; a few yards (meters) of waste yarn and smooth satin ribbon for provisional cast-on; size H/8 (4.75 mm) crochet hook.

Gauge 15 sts and 23 rows = 4" (10 cm) in St st. Exact gauge is not critical for the poncho, but changes in gauge may affect the fit of the beret.

Notes

- The poncho is worked from the neck down, beginning with the ribbed turtleneck. Next, the sawtooth points are worked from side to side around the base of the turtleneck. Finally, the wide bias strips are worked from side to side and shaped with short-rows to flare at the lower edge. The bias strips are worked in alternating bands of stockinette stitch and reverse stockinette stitch. The red accent lines are added in stem stitch embroidery after the knitting is complete.
- The beret is worked upward from the brim, beginning with a ribbed band worked in the round and followed by sawtooth points that are worked from side to side above the band. The crown is shaped with short-row panels of alternating stockinette stitch and reverse stockinette stitch, and embroidered in the same manner as the poncho.

Poncho

Turtleneck

With black and shorter cir needle, CO 100 sts. Place marker (pm) and join for working in the rnd, being careful not to twist sts. Work in k1, p1 rib in the rnd until piece measures 8" (20.5 cm) from CO. Do not BO.

Sawtooth Points

With waste yarn and ribbon, and using the ribbon method provisional cast-on (see Glossary, page 131), CO 10 sts onto a single dpn. Holding the dpn in your left hand, use smaller cir needle with turtleneck sts and black to knit 1 WS row across 10 new CO sts.

Turn work so RS is facing. Work sawtooth points, joining to the live sts at base of turtleneck as foll:

Row 1: (RS) K7, yo, k2, sl 1, k1 from turtleneck, psso—11 sts on dpn; 1 st joined from turtleneck.

Row 2 and all even-numbered rows: (WS) P4, knit to end of sawtooth point sts.

Row 3: K8, yo, k2, sl 1, k1 from turtleneck, psso—12 sts on dpn.

Row 5: K9, yo, k2, sl 1, k1 from turtleneck, psso—13 sts on dpn.

Row 7: K10, yo, k2, sl 1, k1 from turtleneck, psso—14 sts on dpn.

Row 9: K11, yo, k2, sl 1, k1 from turtleneck, psso—15 sts on dpn.

Row 11: K12, yo, k2, sl 1, k1 from turtleneck, psso—16 sts on dpn.

Row 13: K13, yo, k2, sl 1, k1 from turtleneck, psso—17 sts on dpn.

Row 15: K14, yo, k2, sl 1, k1 from turtleneck, psso—18 sts on dpn.

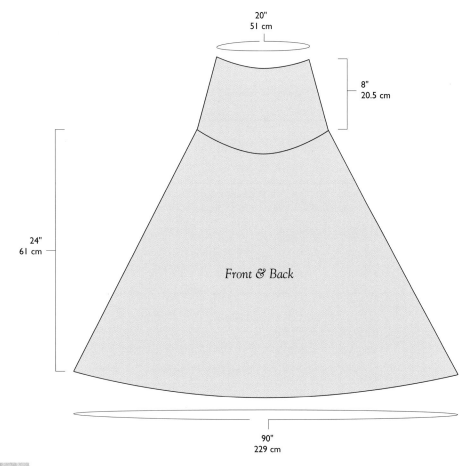

20" / 51 cm

8" / 20.5 cm

24" / 61 cm

Front & Back

90" / 229 cm

Row 17: K15, yo, k2, sl 1, k1 from turtleneck, psso—19 sts on dpn.

Row 19: K16, yo, k2, sl 1, k1 from turtleneck, psso—20 sts on dpn.

Row 20: P4, knit to end.

With RS facing, break yarn, leaving an 8" (20.5-cm) tail to use later for closing up the opening between the bias strip and sawtooth point, and place first 10 sts on holder or waste yarn. Rejoin yarn with RS facing to rem 10 sts. Work Rows 1–20 nine more times, each time placing 10 sts on holder or waste yarn after completing Row 20—10 sts rem on needle after completing 10th sawtooth point; 10 groups of 10 sts each on holders. Carefully remove waste yarn from base of provisional CO, and with black threaded on a tapestry needle, use the Kitchener st (see Glossary, page 134) to graft rem 10 live sts to 10 sts at base of CO for first sawtooth point.

Bias Strips

The lower body is worked from side to side in alternating strips of St st and rev St st. Each strip is joined to the held sts of one sawtooth point. With waste yarn and ribbon, longer cir needle, and using the ribbon method provisional cast-on, CO 90 sts. Join charcoal heather and knit 1 WS row. Work short-rows (see Glossary, page 136) as foll:

Row 1: (RS) K10, wrap next st, turn work around.

Even-numbered Rows 2–16: (WS) Purl to end.

Row 3: Working the wrapped st tog with its wrap as you come to it, k20, wrap next st, turn. On foll RS Rows 5–17, work wrapped st of previous row tog with its wrap as you come to it.

Row 5: K30, wrap next st, turn.

Row 7: K40, wrap next st, turn.

Row 9: K50, wrap next st, turn.

Row 11: K60, wrap next st, turn.

Row 13: K70, wrap next st, turn.

Row 15: K80, wrap next st, turn.

Row 17: K89, sl 1 (last st of strip), place 10 held sts from one sawtooth point on dpn with RS facing, k1 (first sawtooth point st), psso—90 strip sts; 1 st from sawtooth point has been joined.

Row 18: Purl to end.

Odd-numbered Rows 19–35: K89, sl 1, k1 (sawtooth point st), psso, turn. When Row 35 has been completed, all sts of sawtooth point will have been joined—90 strip sts.

Even-numbered Rows 20–34: Purl to end.

Row 36: (WS) BO 10 sts, purl to end—80 strip sts.

Row 37: K70, wrap next st, turn.

Even-numbered Rows 38–50: Purl to end.

Row 39: K60, wrap next st, turn.

Row 41: K50, wrap next st, turn.

Row 43: K40, wrap next st, turn.

Row 45: K30, wrap next st, turn.

Row 47: K20, wrap next st, turn.

Row 49: K10, wrap next st, turn.

Row 51: K80, working all wrapped sts tog with their wraps—80 strip sts.

Row 52: (WS) Knit to end, use the cable method (see Glossary, page 131) to CO 10 sts—90 strip sts.

Rows 53–68: Working in rev St st (purl RS rows; knit WS rows), rep Rows 1–16.

Row 69: P89, sl 1 last st of strip, place 10 held sts from next sawtooth point on dpn with RS facing, k1 (first sawtooth point st), psso—90 strip sts; 1 st from sawtooth point has been joined.

Row 70: Knit to end.

Odd-numbered Rows 71–87: P89, sl 1, k1 (sawtooth point st), psso, turn. When Row 87 has been completed, all sts of sawtooth point will have been joined—90 strip sts.

Even-numbered Rows 72–86: Knit to end.

Row 88: (WS) BO 10 sts, knit to end—80 strip sts.

Row 89: P70, wrap next st, turn.

Even-numbered Rows 90–102: Knit to end.

Row 91: P60, wrap next st, turn.

Row 93: P50, wrap next st, turn.

Row 95: P40, wrap next st, turn.

Row 97: P30, wrap next st, turn.

Row 99: P20, wrap next st, turn.

Row 101: P10, wrap next st, turn.

Row 103: P80, working all wrapped sts tog with their wraps—80 strip sts.

Row 104: (WS) Knit to end, use the cable method to CO 10 sts—90 strip sts.

Rep Rows 1–104 four more times, but do *not* CO 10 sts at end of final Row 104—10 strips completed; sts for all 10 sawtooth points have been joined; 80 live sts on needle. Carefully remove waste yarn from base of provisional CO, and place sts on spare longer cir needle. With RS facing, transfer first 10 sts from base of first strip to holder—80 sts from provisional CO on spare cir needle. With charcoal heather threaded on a tapestry needle, use the Kitchener st to graft 80 sts from base of CO to 80 live sts on main needle.

Finishing

With black tails threaded on a tapestry needle, close short slits where bias strips meet sawtooth points by sewing BO edge of slit to selvedge of adjacent sawtooth point.

Lower Edging

Place held sts from provisional CO on dpn and join charcoal heather with RS to st at end of dpn. With crochet hook, work 1 reverse single crochet st (rev sc; see Glossary, page 132) in each st on dpn to secure sts. Cont to work 1 row of rev sc around bottom edge of poncho, working 2 rev sc for every 3 knitted rows along selvedges and 1 rev sc for every st along horizontal edges. Weave in all loose ends.

Embroidery

With 2 strands of red threaded on a tapestry needle, work a row of stem stitches (see Glossary page 133) along the boundary between each St st and rev St st bias strip—10 rows of embroidery total.

Wash in cold water with mild soap or shampoo and rinse with hair conditioner. Lay flat to dry. When slightly damp, lightly steam-block.

Beret

Ribbing

With black and dpn, CO 72 sts. Arrange sts evenly on 3 or 4 dpn, place marker (pm), and join for working in the rnd, being careful not to twist sts. Work k1, p1 rib until piece measures 1½" (3.8 cm) from CO. Do not BO. Break yarn.

Sawtooth Points

With waste yarn and ribbon, and using the ribbon method provisional cast-on (see Glossary, page 131), CO 4 sts onto dpn at end of last ribbing rnd. Turn work, and with WS facing, rejoin yarn to beg of CO sts, knit across the 4 newly CO sts. Cont with black, work sawtooth points, joining to the live sts at top edge of ribbing as foll:

Row 1: (RS) K3, yo, sl 1, k1 from ribbing, psso—5 sawtooth point sts.

Row 2 and all even-numbered rows through Row 10: (WS) Knit to end of sawtooth point sts.

Row 3: K4, yo, sl 1, k1 from ribbing, psso—6 sawtooth point sts.

Row 5: K5, yo, sl 1, k1 from

ribbing, psso—7 sawtooth point sts.

Row 7: K6, yo, sl 1, k1 from ribbing, psso—8 sawtooth point sts.

Row 9: K7, yo, sl 1, k1 from ribbing, psso—9 sawtooth point sts.

Row 11: BO 6 sts (1 st rem on right-hand needle), k1, yo, sl 1, k1 from ribbing, psso—4 sawtooth point sts; 6 ribbing sts joined.

Rows 12: (WS) Knit to end of sawtooth point sts.

Rep Rows 1–12 eleven more times—4 sts rem on sawtooth point needle after completing 12th sawtooth point; all sts of ribbing have been joined. Carefully remove waste yarn from base of provisional CO and with black threaded on a tapestry needle, graft rem 4 live sts to 4 sts at base of CO (see Glossary, page 134).

Bias Strips

With dpn, pick up 6 sts along selvedge of one sawtooth point (1 st for each garter ridge); these sts are just picked up by slipping the needle into the edge loops, not picked up and knitted. With shorter cir needle, waste yarn and ribbon, and using the ribbon method provisional cast-on, CO 24 sts. Join charcoal heather to 24 sts on cir needle with RS facing.

Work short-rows (see Glossary, page 136) as foll:

Row 1: (RS) K24, with RS facing pick up and knit 6 sts along horizontal BO edge of sawtooth point at the base of the picked-up sts on the dpn, k1 from dpn, pass 2nd st on right-hand needle over, turn—30 strip sts; 1 st joined from dpn.

Row 2: Purl to last 4 sts, wrap next st, turn work around.

Row 3: Knit to last strip st, sl 1, k1 from dpn, psso, turn.

Row 4: Purl to 4 sts before wrapped st of previous WS row, wrap next st, turn.

Rows 5–10: Rep Rows 3 and 4 three more times—5 wrapped sts total; 5 sts joined from dpn; with RS facing, wrapped st of Row 10 is the 20th st of row.

Row 11: Knit to last strip st, sl 1, k1 from dpn, psso, turn—all dpn sts joined.

Row 12: P8 (2 sts before wrapped st), p2tog, purl wrapped st tog with its wrap, [p1, p2tog, purl wrapped st tog with its wrap] 4 times, p1, p2tog—24 strip sts. With dpn, pick up 6 sts along selvedge of next sawtooth point.

Rows 13–24: Working in rev St st (purl RS rows; knit WS rows), rep Rows 1–12.

Rep Rows 1–24 five more times;

there will not be a sawtooth selvedge to pick up sts from after the final Row 12—12 bias strips completed; edges of all 12 sawtooth points have been joined; 24 live sts on needle. Carefully remove waste yarn from base of provisional CO and place sts on another cir. With charcoal heather threaded on a tapestry needle, use the Kitchener st to graft 24 sts from base of CO to 24 live sts.

Finishing

With charcoal heather threaded on a tapestry needle, tighten up the hole at the center of the crown as much as possible. Weave in all loose ends. With 2 strands of red threaded on a tapestry needle, work a row of stem stitches (see Glossary page 133) along the boundary between every other pair of St st and rev St st bias strips—6 rows of embroidery total.

Wash in cold water with mild soap or shampoo and rinse with hair conditioner. Lay flat to dry. When slightly damp, lightly steam-block on an 11" (28-cm) form such as a dinner plate or circle of stiff cardboard.

GLOSSARY

Abbreviations

beg	begin(s); beginning
BO	bind off
CC	contrast color
cm	centimeter(s)
cn	cable needle
CO	cast on
dec(s)	decrease(s); decreasing
dpn	double-pointed needles
g	gram(s)
inc(s)	increase(s); increasing
k	knit
k1f&b	knit into the front and back of same st
kwise	knitwise; as if to knit
m	marker(s)
MC	main color
mm	millimeter(s)
M1	make one (increase)
p	purl
p1f&b	purl into front and back of same st
patt(s)	pattern(s)
psso	pass slipped st over
pwise	purlwise, as if to purl
rem	remain(s); remaining
rep	repeat(s); repeating
rev St st	reverse stockinette stitch
rnd(s)	round(s)
RS	right side
sl	slip
sl st	slip st (slip st pwise unless otherwise indicated)
ssk	slip 2 sts kwise, one at a time, from the left needle to right needle, insert left needle tip through both front loops and knit together from this position (1 st decrease)
St st	stockinette stitch
tbl	through back loop
tog	together
WS	wrong side
wyb	with yarn in back
wyf	with yarn in front
yd	yard(s)
yo	yarnover
*	repeat starting point
**	repeat all instructions between asterisks
( )	alternate measurements and/or instructions
[ ]	instructions are worked as a group a specified number of times.

Bind-Offs

Standard Bind-Off

Knit the first stitch, *knit the next stitch (2 stitches on right needle), insert left needle tip into first stitch on right needle (Figure 1) and lift this stitch up and over the second stitch (Figure 2) and off the needle (Figure 3). Repeat from * for the desired number of stitches.

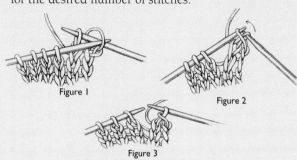

Figure 1

Figure 2

Figure 3

Sewn K1 P1 Rib Bind-Off

Cut the yarn three times the width of the knitting to be bound off and thread it on a tapestry needle. Working from right to left, insert tapestry needle purlwise (from right to left) through the first (knit) stitch (Figure 1) and pull the yarn through. Bring tapestry needle behind the knit stitch, insert it knitwise (from left to right) into the second (purl) stitch (Figure 2) and pull the yarn through. *Slip the first knit stitch knitwise off the knitting needle, insert tapestry needle purlwise into the next knit stitch (Figure 3) and pull the yarn through, slip the first stitch purlwise off the knitting needle, then bring the tapestry needle behind the knit stitch, insert it knitwise into the next purl stitch (Figure 4), and pull the yarn through. Repeat from * for the desired number of stitches.

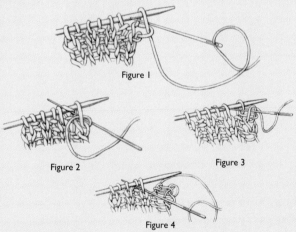

Figure 1

Figure 2

Figure 3

Figure 4

Cast-Ons

Backward Loop Cast-On

Leaving a short end, make a slipknot on the needle.
*Tension the yarn in your left hand and make a loop around your thumb, insert the needle in the loop, slip your thumb out, and gently pull the yarn to form a stitch on the needle. Repeat from * for the desired number of stitches.

Cable Cast-On

Hold needle with working yarn in your left hand with the wrong side of the work facing you. *Insert right needle *between* the first 2 stitches on left needle (Figure 1), wrap yarn around needle as if to knit, draw yarn through (Figure 2), and place new loop on left needle (Figure 3) to form a new stitch. Repeat from * for the desired number of stitches, always working between the first 2 stitches on the left needle.

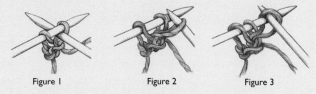

Figure 1   Figure 2   Figure 3

Knitted Cast-On

Make a slipknot of working yarn and place it on the left needle if there are no stitches already there. *Use the right needle to knit the first stitch (or slipknot) on left needle (Figure 1) and place new loop onto left needle to form a new stitch (Figure 2). Repeat from * for the desired number of stitches, always working into the last stitch made.

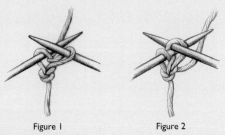

Figure 1   Figure 2

Long-Tail Cast-On

Leaving a long tail (about ½" [1.3 cm] for each stitch to be cast on), make a slipknot and place it on the right needle. Place thumb and index finger of your left hand between the yarn ends so that working yarn is around your index finger and tail end is around your thumb. Secure the yarn ends with your other fingers and hold your palm upwards,

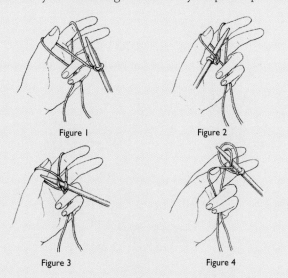

Figure 1   Figure 2

Figure 3   Figure 4

making a V of yarn (Figure 1). *Bring needle up through loop on thumb (Figure 2), catch first strand around index finger, and go back down through loop on thumb (Figure 3). Drop loop off thumb and, placing thumb back in V configuration, tighten resulting stitch on needle (Figure 4). Repeat from * for the desired number of stitches.

Removable (Provisional) Cast-On

Make a loose slipknot of working yarn and place it on the right needle. Hold a length of waste yarn next to the slipknot and around your left thumb; hold working yarn over your left index finger. *Bring right needle forward under waste yarn, over working yarn, grab a loop of working yarn (Figure 1), then bring needle to the front over both yarns and grab a second loop (Figure 2). Repeat from * for the desired number of stitches. When you're ready to work in the opposite direction, place the exposed loops on a knitting needle as you pull out the waste yarn.

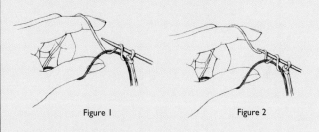

Figure 1   Figure 2

Ribbon Method Provisional Cast-On

With smooth waste yarn, use the long-tail method (at left) to cast on the desired number of stitches. Knit 1 row, then purl 1 row. Leaving a long tail at the beginning of the row, knit the next row with a contrasting color of ⅛" (3 mm) wide smooth satin ribbon. Cut the ribbon, leaving another long tail at the end of the row. Beginning with the next row, use the working yarn to work the pattern as specified in the instructions (Figure 1). When you're ready to work in the opposite direction, place the exposed loops of the working yarn on a knitting needle as you pull out the ribbon (Figure 2). Discard the ribbon and waste-yarn stitches.

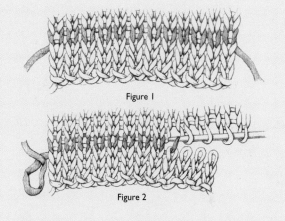

Figure 1

Figure 2

Crochet

Crochet Chain (ch)

Make a slipknot and place it on a crochet hook. *Yarn over hook and draw through loop on hook. Repeat from * for the desired number of stitches. To fasten off, cut yarn and draw end through last loop formed.

Double Crochet (dc)

*Yarn over hook, insert hook into the fourth chain from hook or next stitch, yarn over hook and draw through a loop (3 loops on hook), yarn over hook (Figure 1) and draw it through 2 loops, yarn over hook and draw it through remaining 2 loops (Figure 2). Repeat from * for the desired number of stitches. At the end of the row, chain 3 stitches and turn the work around. Begin the next row by inserting the hook into the last stitch of previous row.

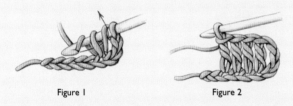

Figure 1   Figure 2

Half Double Crochet (hdc)

*Yarn over hook, insert hook into the third chain from hook or next stitch, yarn over hook and draw through a loop (3 loops on hook), yarn over hook (Figure 1) and draw it through all loops on hook (Figure 2). Repeat from * for the desired number of stitches. At the end of the row, chain 2 stitches and turn the work around. Begin the next row by inserting the hook into the last stitch of previous row.

Figure 1   Figure 2

Quadruple Crochet (qc)

*Yarn over hook 3 times, insert the hook in the sixth chain from the hook or next stitch, yarn over hook and draw through a loop (5 loops on hook; Figure 1), yarn over hook and draw it through 2 loops (Figure 2), yarn over hook and draw it through the next 2 loops (Figure 3), yarn over hook

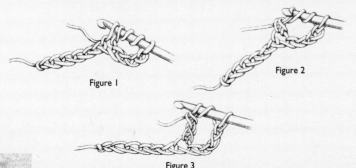

Figure 1   Figure 2

Figure 3

draw it through next 2 loops (Figure 4), yarnover hook and draw it through remaining loops (Figure 5). Repeat from * for the desired number of stitches. At the end of the row, chain 5 stitches and turn the work around. Begin the next row by inserting the hook into the last stitch of previous row.

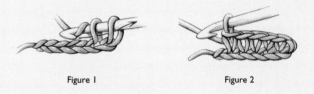

Figure 4   Figure 5

Single Crochet (sc)

*Insert hook into the second chain from hook or next stitch, yarn over hook and draw through a loop, yarn over hook (Figure 1), and draw it through both loops on hook (Figure 2). Repeat from * for the desired number of stitches. At the end of the row, chain 2 stitches and turn the work around. Begin the next row by inserting the hook into the last stitch of previous row.

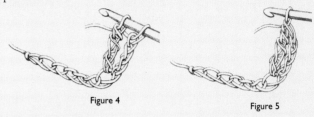

Figure 1   Figure 2

Slip Stitch Crochet (sl st)

*Insert hook into stitch, yarn over hook and draw a loop through both the stitch and loop already on hook. Repeat from * for the desired number of stitches.

Reverse Single Crochet (shrimp st)

Working from left to right, insert hook into a stitch, draw through a loop, bring yarn over hook, and draw it through the first one. *Insert hook into next stitch to the right (Figure 1), draw through a loop, bring yarn over hook again (Figure 2), and draw it through both loops on hook. Repeat from * for the desired number of stitches (Figure 3).

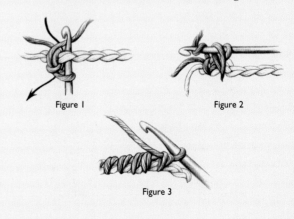

Figure 1   Figure 2

Figure 3

Treble Crochet (tr)

*Yarn over hook 2 times, insert hook into the fifth chain from hook or next stitch, yarn over hook and draw through a loop (4 loops on hook; Figure 1), yarn over hook and draw it through 2 loops (Figure 2), yarn over hook and draw it through the next 2 loops, yarn over hook and draw it through the remaining 2 loops (Figure 3). Repeat from * for the desired number of stitches. At the end of the row, chain 4 stitches and turn the work around. Begin the next row by inserting the hook into the last stitch of previous row.

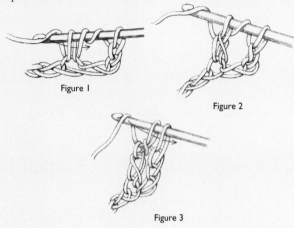

Figure 1

Figure 2

Figure 3

Decreases

K2tog

Knit 2 stitches together as if they were a single stitch.

Ssk

Slip 2 stitches individually knitwise (Figure 1), insert left needle tip into the front of these 2 slipped stitches, and use the right needle to knit them together through their back loops (Figure 2).

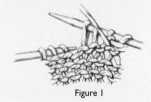

Figure 1

Figure 2

Ssp

Holding yarn in front, slip 2 stitches individually knitwise (Figure 1), then slip these 2 stitches back onto left needle (they will appear twisted) and purl them together through their back loops (Figure 2).

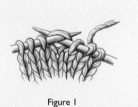

Figure 1

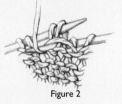

Figure 2

Embroidery

Backstitch

Bring threaded needle out from back to front between 2 knitted stitches. Insert needle at the right edge of the right stitch, then back out at the left edge of the left stitch. Insert needle again between the first 2 stitches and bring it out 2 stitches to the left. Continue in this manner, working 1 stitch to the right and 2 stitches to the left in a circular motion.

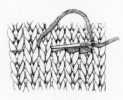

Buttonhole Stitch

Working into edge half-stitch of the knitted piece, *bring tip of threaded needle in and out of a knitted stitch, place working yarn under needle tip, then bring threaded needle through the stitch and tighten. Repeat from *, always bringing threaded needle on top of working yarn.

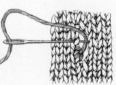

Chain Stitch

Bring threaded needle out from back to front at the center of a knitted stitch. *Form a short loop and insert needle back where it came out. Keeping the loop under the needle, bring the needle back out in the center of the next knitted stitch. Repeat from * for the desired number of stitches.

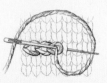

Duplicate Stitch

Bring threaded needle out from back to front at the base of the V of the knitted stitch you want to cover. Working right to left, *pass needle in and out under the stitch in the row above it and back into the base of the same stitch. Bring needle back out at the base of the V in the next stitch to be covered. Repeat from * for the desired number of stitches.

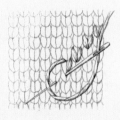

Mosaic Stitch

This stitch is worked on the diagonal on woven Aida cloth. Work 1 line of stitches that covers every intersection of threads in the base cloth. Work the adjacent line of stitches over 2 intersections at a time. Alternate between diagonal lines of short and long stitches.

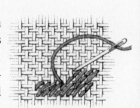

Stem Stitch

*Bring threaded needle out of knitted background from back, then back into the background a short distance away, then out again a short distance below. Repeat from * for desired length.

Wicker Stitch

This stitch is worked on woven Aida cloth. Working vertically, bring threaded tapestry needle across 4 adjacent threads 4 times (Figure 1), then work horizontally across the next 4 threads 4 times. Alternate between groups of 4 vertical and 4 horizontal stitches (Figure 2).

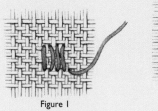 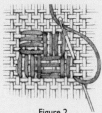

Figure 1   Figure 2

Woven Stitch

This stitch is worked in two parts on a background of knitted fabric. *Bring threaded tapestry needle over the right half of the V of the stitch to be covered, then under the left half of the same stitch. Repeat from * for each stitch along the row to be covered, pulling the thread until it is snug without causing puckers (Figure 1). Work another pass across the same row of stitches in the opposite direction, this time covering the parts of the stitches not covered in the first pass (Figure 2).

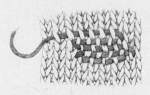 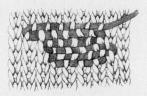

Figure 1   Figure 2

Fair Isle Knitting

Hold and work with one yarn in the right hand in the usual way (Figure 1). Tension the other yarn through the fingers of your left hand. To knit with the left-hand yarn, insert the right needle, dip it under the yarn, and pull it through with a hook-like action (Figure 2). At the beginning of each new row, make sure to tension the yarn that is going to be used the most on your right hand. As you knit with the right-hand yarn 3 or more sts, make sure the left-hand yarn is woven over and under on alternate sts on the WS, taking care the contrast color does not show through to the RS.

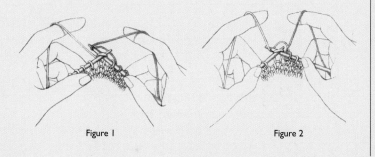

Figure 1   Figure 2

Grafting

Graft Live Stitches to Bound-Off or Cast-On Edge (backstitch)

Allowing about ½" (1.3 cm) per stitch to be grafted, thread matching yarn on a tapestry needle. Work from right to left as follows:

Step 1. Bring tapestry needle up under first stitch of bound-off or cast-on edge and through the first stitch on the needle as if to purl.

Step 2. Bring tapestry needle down through the same stitch on bound-off or cast-on edge, up under the next stitch to the left (Figure 2).

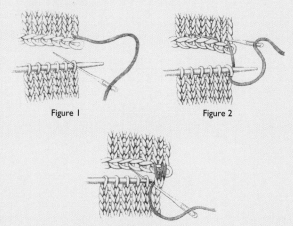

Figure 1   Figure 2

Figure 3

Step 3. Bring tapestry needle through the first stitch on the needle as if to knit, slip this stitch off the needle, then bring tapestry needle through the next stitch on needle as if to purl and leave this stitch on the needle (Figure 3). Repeat Steps 2 and 3 until no stitches remain.

Graft Live Stitches to Live Stitches (Kitchener stitch)

Arrange stitches on 2 needles so that there is the same number of stitches on each needle. Hold the needles parallel to each other with right sides of the knitting facing up. Allowing about ½" (1.3 cm) per stitch to be grafted, thread matching yarn on a tapestry needle. Work from right to left as follows:

Step 1. Bring tapestry needle through the first stitch on the front needle as if to purl and leave the stitch on the needle (Figure 1).

Step 2. Bring tapestry needle through the first stitch on the back needle as if to knit and leave that stitch on the needle (Figure 2).

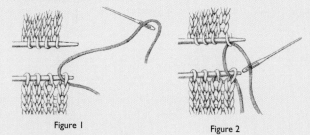

Figure 1   Figure 2

Step 3. Bring tapestry needle through the first front stitch as if to knit and slip this stitch off the needle, then bring seaming needle through the next front stitch as if to purl and leave this stitch on the needle (Figure 3).

Step 4. Bring tapestry needle through the first back stitch as if to purl and slip this stitch off the needle, then bring tapestry needle through the next back stitch as if to knit and leave this stitch on the needle (Figure 4).

Repeat Steps 3 and 4 until no stitches remain on the needles, adjusting the tension to match the rest of the knitting.

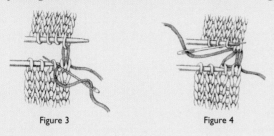

Figure 3   Figure 4

Graft Live Stitches to Knitted Rows (hems)

Fold hem facing to garment so that wrong sides are facing together. Allowing about ½" (1.3 cm) per stitch to be grafted, thread matching yarn on a tapestry needle. With wrong side of garment facing, work from right to left as follows:

Step 1. Bring threaded needle down through center of 1 live stitch, then up through center of next live stitch (Figure 1).

Step 2. Catch both legs of corresponding stitch on knitted fabric, being careful not to bring seaming thread to the right side of the work (Figure 2).

Repeat Steps 1 and 2, matching the path of a knitted row.

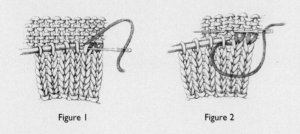

Figure 1   Figure 2

I-Cord

Using 2 double-pointed needles, cast on the desired number of stitches (usually 3 to 4). *Without turning the needle, slide stitches to other end of needle, pull the yarn around the back, and knit the stitches as usual. Repeat from * for desired length.

Increases

K1f&b

Knit into a stitch but leave the stitch on the left needle (Figure 1), then knit through the back loop of the same stitch (Figure 2) and slip the original stitch off the needle.

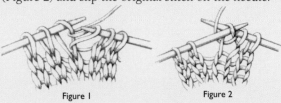

Figure 1   Figure 2

Make One (M1)

With left needle tip, lift the strand between last knitted stitch and first stitch on left needle from front to back (Figure 1), then knit the lifted loop through the back (Figure 2).

Figure 1   Figure 2

P1f&b

Purl into a stitch but leave that stich on the left needle (Figure 1), then purl through the back loop of the same stitch (Figure 2) and slip the original stitch off the needle.

Figure 1   Figure 2

Intarsia

Intarsia Knitting

On knit rows, knit to the color change, drop the working yarn, pick up the second color, bringing it around the first yarn before knitting the next stitch (Figure 1). On purl rows, purl to the color change, drop the working yarn, then pick up the next color, bringing it over the previous yarn (Figure 2). For optimum results and to avoid tangles, always twist the first color *over* the second color on knit rows and twist the first color *under* the second on purl rows.

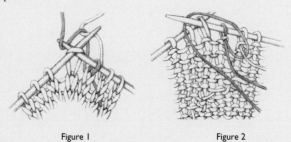

Figure 1   Figure 2

Pick Up and Knit

Work from right to left with right side facing. For horizontal (bind-off or cast-on) edges: Insert tip of needle into the center of the stitch below the bind-off or cast-on edge (Figure 1), wrap yarn around needle, and pull it through to make a stitch on the needle (Figure 2). Pick up 1 stitch for every stitch along the horizontal edge. For shaped edges, insert needle between last and second-to-last stitches, wrap yarn around needle, and pull it through to make a stitch on the needle (Figure 3). Pick up about 3 stitches for every 4 rows along shaped edges.

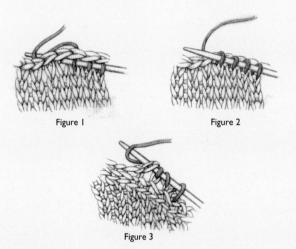

Figure 1   Figure 2

Figure 3

Seams

Backstitch Seam

Hold pieces to be seamed so that their right sides face each other and so that the edges to be seamed are even with each other. Thread seaming yarn on a tapestry needle and join the pieces as follows: *Insert threaded needle through both layers, from back to front, 2 stitches to the left (Figure 1), then from front to back 1 stitch to the right (Figure 2). Repeat from * for desired seam length, working right to left so that seaming yarn follows a circular path.

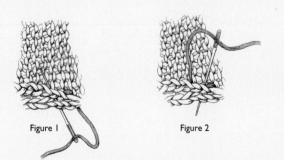

Figure 1   Figure 2

Slipstitch Seam

Make a slipknot with seaming yarn and place on crochet hook. With right sides of pieces facing each other, *insert hook through both pieces of fabric under the stitch loops, wrap yarn around hook to form a loop (Figure 1), and pull loop back through both pieces of fabric and through the loop already on hook (Figure 2). Repeat from * for desired seam length, maintaining firm, even tension.

Figure 1   Figure 2

Whipstitch Seam

Working in a circular motion from right to left, bring threaded tapestry needle through purl bump on wrong side of knitted fabric, then through edge of facing.

Short-Rows

Work to turning point, slip next stitch purlwise to right needle, then bring the yarn to the front (Figure 1). Slip the same stitch back to the left needle (Figure 2), turn the work around and bring the yarn in position for the next stitch, wrapping the slipped stitch with working yarn as you do so. When you come to a wrapped stitch on a subsequent row, hide the wrap by working it together with the wrapped stitch as follows: Insert right needle tip under the wrap (from the front if wrapped stitch is a knit stitch; from the back if wrapped stitch is a purl stitch), then into the stitch on the needle, and work the stitch and its wrap together as a single stitch.

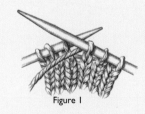
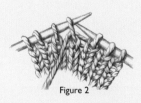

Figure 1   Figure 2

Resources

The Alpaca Yarn Company
144 Roosevelt Ave.
Bay #1
York, PA 17401
www.thealpacayarnco.com
Classic Alpaca
Suri Elegance

Alpaca With a Twist
4272 Evans Jacobi Rd.
Georgetown, IN 47122
www.AlpacaWithATwist.com
Baby Twist

America's Alpaca (See The Alpaca
Yarn Company)

Bead Station
24412-A Muirlands
Lake Forest, CA 92630
www.beadstn.com
Toho Beads

Classic Elite Yarns
122 Western Ave.
Lowell, MA 01851
www.classiceliteyarns.com
Premiere

The DMC Corporation
107 Trumbull St.
Elizabeth, NJ 07206
www.dmc-usa.com
#3 Perle Cotton

The Fibre Company
144 Fore St.
Studio D-1
Portland, ME 04101
www.TheFibreCo.com
Black Lace
Starry Night
White Diamond
Zorro

JHB International
1955 South Quince St.
Denver, CO 80231
www.buttons.com

Lanart
202 S. Old Statesville Rd.
Huntersville, NC 28078
Suri Alpaca Fur

Plymouth Yarn Company
PO Box 28
Bristol, PA 19007
www.plymouthyarn.com
Baby Alpaca Grande

Trendsetter Yarns
16745 Saticoy St. #101
Van Nuys, CA 91406
www.trendsetteryarns.com
Segue

Bibliography

Jose Antonio de Lavalle. *Huari.* Coleccion Arte y Tesoros del Peru. Lima: Banco de Credito del Peru en la Cultura, 1984.

————, and Rosario de Lavalle de Cardenas. *Tejidos Milenarios del Peru/ Ancient Peruvian Textiles.* Lima: AFP Integra, 1999.

————, and Werner Lang. *Chancay* Coleccion Arte y Tesoros del Peru. Lima: Banco de Credito del Peru en la Cultura, 1982.

Index

abbreviations 130
alpacas, breeding 115; evolution 31

bind-offs 130
Black and White Handbag 44–47
Bohemian Poncho and Beret 124–129
Bolero 116–123

camelids 31
camels 31
cast-ons 130–131
ceremonial dress 83
Chancay 59, 61, 65, 75, 79, 85, 91, 99, 117
Circular Cardigan with Tapestry Weaving 98–105
cloth see textiles, Peruvian
clothing, traditional 83
costume see clothing, traditional
crochet stitches 132–133
Crocheted Poncho 60–63

decreases 133
dress see clothing, traditional

Embroidered-Back Cardigan and Crocheted Beads 48–57
Embroidered Yoke Wrap and Crocheted Cloche 2–11
embroidery stitches 133–134

Fair Isle knitting 134

Geometric Scarf 112–114
glossary 130–136
grafting 134–135
guanacos 31

Huari 23, 33, 46, 58

I-cord 135
Inca 59
Incan Pachacamac 107
increases 135
intarsia 135

Lacy Shawl with Fur Trim 74–77
Lambayeque 49, 59
llamas 31, 59
Lliclla 79–83
Long Asymmetrical Cardigan 22–30

map, Peru 1

Nazca 13, 23, 58

Paracus 3, 58
Patwork Kimono and Beaded Cap 32–43
Peru; cultural evolution 58–59
pick up and knit 136

Ropp, Carol A. 115

seams 136
Short Asymmetrical Jacket and Flower Pin 12–20
Short Cape 106–111
Short Cardigan with Ribbon Trim 64–73
Short Circular Cardigan 90–97
short-rows 136
Spanish 59
stitches, crochet 132–133; embroidery 133–134
Striped Pullover and Spiral Scarf 84–89
suppliers, yarn 137
Suri fur 75

Tanasi Trace Alpacas 115
textiles, Peruvian 21, 58

vicuñas 31, 59

Winsauer, Sharon 65, 75

yarn suppliers 137